Being the
Phoenix

Dennis Arbour

BALBOA.
PRESS

A DIVISION OF HAY HOUSE

Balboa Press books may be ordered through booksellers or by contacting:

Balboa Press
A Division of Hay House
1663 Liberty Drive
Bloomington, IN 47403
www.balboapress.com
1 (877) 407-4847

Because of the dynamic nature of the Internet, any web addresses or links contained in this book may have changed since publication and may no longer be valid. The views expressed in this work are solely those of the author and do not necessarily reflect the views of the publisher, and the publisher hereby disclaims any responsibility for them.

The author of this book does not dispense medical advice or prescribe the use of any technique as a form of treatment for physical, emotional, or medical problems without the advice of a physician, either directly or indirectly. The intent of the author is only to offer information of a general nature to help you in your quest for emotional and spiritual well-being. In the event you use any of the information in this book for yourself, which is your constitutional right, the author and the publisher assume no responsibility for your actions.

Any people depicted in stock imagery provided by Thinkstock are models, and such images are being used for illustrative purposes only.
Certain stock imagery © Thinkstock.

Printed in the United States of America.

ISBN: 978-1-4525-8735-6 (sc)
ISBN: 978-1-4525-8736-3 (e)

Library of Congress Control Number: 2013921444

Balboa Press rev. date: 12/13/2013

Contents

"The most extraordinary thing that happened
in my life was dying.
The next most extraordinary thing that happened
Was returning. I fear death no more."

=\7/=

(1)

Higher Realities

I held my hands up with palms out and examined my fingernails that had taken on a strange oddity. The sun through the window on them showed something like a nail that had been damaged by a blow and stopped growing, and behind was coming in a new growth. But unlike a true blow to the nails, there was no darkened area as would be found in pounding one's thumb with a hammer. It was more a delineation where the old nail was defined from a new nail's growth. On both my hands the same was evident and on every nail. I took my shoes and socks off and found that all my toes were the same. They all had a stop and then start to their growth. My curiosity led me to finding out how long it takes to entirely grow a nail either on the hands or the feet, and then carefully examining how far the nails had grown at this current time. By their growth, they matched a recent and particular time of my being in an intensive care unit under a ventilator, and seemingly to a medical staff, I was dying. All that could be done had been done and all was fallen into the hands of God.

I survived that moment that was about the eighth or ninth day in a sixteen day period, finally coming to consciousness in the end. A little while down the road in time I discovered my fingernails and came to a conclusion: I had died and then had come back, returning with an amazing and unforgettable "vision" just before

1

fully awakening. Upon my hands and feet was a physical proof that I had died, then returned.

Many times I have re-examined the vision received during the coma I was in while hospitalized. I still find it astonishing and very profound, and an experience I am compelled to share. I was given my life back and bidden to return to this that we call the land of the Living. From this vision, and other things that I saw and was shown and told, I know in myself much of what I could have never gained in this lifetime without such an experience. So perhaps this experience is not simply for me alone, as it has touched on the lives of so many around me and shall continue to do so. Often now when this story is told there comes a look of astonishment on those who hear, and a sense of hope and faith is rekindled, in spite of the dark areas of it as a journey by one individual. I maintain that this is a story of many rather than a single person. It is not unusual that an individual may be called upon to become a living guidepost for others, or an inspiration and strength in the confusions or tragedies of this world. Some of the people around me became such when I was in dire and fearful straits through my journey, so this is not just another story about simply another individual, but of many.

In spite of the tragedies involved, there was an "air" about what happened that made those around me react like a conduit of something greater. Something that we could call "divine" in it's nature that we respond to and brings out the higher in us. We recognize "that something" in ourselves as a strength, beyond the trappings of religion or social protocols. We align with the voice of our spirit within us and do, or help, veritable miracles to occur. It is at that moment that we remember the greater things that do not fit easily into this world nowadays, but are written within us as the memory of a truth from an eternal angle. We all seem to know what beauty is without being taught, for instance. We also have dreams and then awaken and remember them, yet say to each other that although dreams are a reality, they are not real. In that we would be suggesting that this physical existence is all that there is with none above nor below. Again, though, there often comes along an individual who has an experience and shares it that affects others on a scale that is breathtaking and uplifting. It enhances us all to remember we individually have personal experiences that show a shared reality that does not fit well into our worldly view. I ask you to remember that it is challenging to balance such an experience if you are the individual.

Having been through a near death experience, I often have found myself stricken with awe again when it floats into my mind even as a memory. After a period of months, some things that I remember as "dreams" and detached from the initial vision now are seen as a very importantly part of the vision. Whereas one could speculate that as time passes things would seem more muddled and forgotten, the upwellings of memory would suddenly surface a forgotten part and be very clear. For this reason I carried a voice recorder to catch these sudden recollections. Yet a question arose as to how one could remember such a grouping of dreams so vividly and retain them in the face of a non-functioning body in coma. In spite of being biologically curtailed from functioning in the physical world, consciousness and sensory ability still continued on, but on another level of reality.

This is a fascinating aspect of us that clearly shows that consciousness functions above and beyond the body, revealing that consciousness is not a creation of it. And so the separation of dream from "vision" became compelling to understand where I had gone, what I had seen and what the "vision's" content meant, as well as it's credentials as an experience of a higher reality.

A Near Death Experience leaves the individual in a state of recognizing higher levels of reality while also living in this one. It makes one feel that others are "blind" while one can "see". It makes it a subject hard to broach unless there has been some true and unusual experience previously had by a listener. The sudden but short experience of the return of a "dearly departed" loved one, dreams of flying, precognition of events beforehand, hunches that prove to be absolutely correct and many other experiences draw our attention to that inner and upper existence we impinge on. In the telling of such astonishing stories to others, it often happens that many things "come together" to form a greater understanding in the one who was the listener. Their speculations on their own personal experiences that have happened to them suddenly make sense, especially when another reveals such things have happened to them also, in spite of the fact it does not conform with the world at large. Internally, a switch gets flipped that increases our awareness to more subtle levels impinging on this world each and every day. Odd occurrences begin to be noted not as mere "coincidences" but as something "sensed" at a new and deeper level of ourselves. Science deals with the physicality of existence but can only go so far, for the spiritual is not of a physical nature.

We can live in the deeply material nature of the human animal, or we can discover the greater part of ourselves waiting to grow beyond that human animal we "think" we are. That is the very meaning of life as a human being, to grow towards a place we call the "heavens". I broach no religious beliefs, but rather a deep spiritual conviction from inner "eyes that see and ears that hear" in a way that the reader will certainly recognize. And if so, you have found the doorway within yourself to a greater creation than can ever be imagined.

Of course there are some aspects of a near death experience of which I found hard to rectify and caused me to question their content. One such thing was certain envisionments, dreams that were of a decidedly negative nature to see, and made me doubt at times their value. One day, as I pondered the nature of these negative envisionments, I had a sudden and unexpected "coincidence" occur that offered explanation as to their inclusion. I came into the knowledge of the existence of "the Gospel of Mary Magdalena", where Jesus explained to Mary the path in death arriving to heaven being fraught with both demonic and divine beings. One's choice and reaction to this is, seemingly, noted by those who constantly watch over us, the content of our heart steering where we end up. That I would be pondering such a thing and then have such a hint surface to me was, in my eyes, far more than "coincidence". It suggested also that the "heavens" is a state of being rather than a place, although there is such a place. To think and dwell in the negative will attract, and attract you TO, the negative. To think and dwell in the positive will attract, and attract you TO, the positive. We attune ourselves to the level that we are personally creating by choice. This was the lesson learned by "coincidence", the Universe seemingly answering a question of profound depth "out of the blue". It is one of the things that happen daily that a renewed sensitivity will "see and hear".

So now I shall go forward with the course of events that brought me to a life defining moment. Perhaps the reason such events occur is to remind not just the individual, but also all around, that we are invited to reclaim great and divine things.

(2)

The Invisible Tiger

An ambulance took me to the local hospital. Increasingly, over a two week period and just before Thanksgiving, I found that I could not walk well, then not at all and was haunted by a constant back pain.

At the emergency room I entered a battery of tests, a gauntlet for the search of what may be wrong. The MRI was the worst. Not simply because of the noise, but because something "odd" was occurring while in the unit itself. It is one thing to be stuffed in a tube that is very claustrophobic, but at interludes a shock could be felt akin to the type we get from a rug to a doorknob. After the first twenty minute scan and as I was pulled out for a break, I commented on this very uncomfortable experience. The techs looked at each other and then said, "That puts you in a small category of people who build up a charge and it discharges to the walls inside the tube of the MRI".

The next twenty minutes were the same and I was glad when it was over, but I noted this oddity and hoped that another MRI would not be in the future. It certainly compounded my anxiety and fears of what may be wrong with me with such an unusual experience. From there, to x-ray, to blood tests and on, the day was spent, and the sun flew overhead and finished its course. I was now tired, worried and patiently on the edge of despair.

The doctor in the emergency room was kindly, well mannered and very serious when he came into the room. A look on his face warned me to brace myself in what he was about to say. "I have bad news", he said.

Well that was the bad news: That there was bad news. I waited for him to give me explanation while inside of me a strange relief settled in to my heart and thinking. The answer would be known and I would put on the armor to bear a hard course. But I did not expect the doctor to say what he said. And what he said caused a sudden and very fast thought process to unfold within me.

"You seem to have cancer of the spine", said the doctor. "We are going to transport you down to Portland where they can deal with this in their cancer center". The invisible tiger that was eating me alive was revealed. The battle was on. You can speculate what I would be thinking and feeling in that moment, but my thoughts surprised even me. Call it "intuitive" or a sensing that this was not completely and exactly the whole story in a nutshell, but what I thought was "another" explanation. I sensed that what was happening was caused by cancer, yes, but from another source that had spread to my spine. Prostate cancer had been in my family, and was now showing up in my own personal gene pool. But I said not a word because it was best for the circumstance to play itself out and the professionals to further review the situation. I was shipped to the cancer care unit in Portland.

The next morning, I received another MRI, much to my consternation. But I did bring up the odd factor of the static charge and was surprised when they put around me "buffers" to insulate the shocks from happening. Getting through this without more shocks was a blessing in my book, but afterwards and for weeks to come anyone who touched me would get a shock from static. I had no explanation for this.

The battleground composed for combating the "invisible tiger" became a barrage of pills and drugs and the coming and going of nurses and doctors left me in a muddled state. I would wake in the night and feel terror and despair well up in me. I was in a face to face struggle with "the Tiger". This was the first few days that I was there. Those days were naked and grey in feeling, a time when I never felt so alone and uncertain in life. How bad was it? Would I survive? Was my paralysis from the waist down permanent? Was I going to die? And if I lived, would I not walk again? Where just mere weeks ago I could walk and run, dance, climb and stand, I now did'nt even know how to get into a wheelchair. Let alone out of a bed. My prior life was turning to ashes.

This is a time that many others before me had faced, and I wondered where they had found their strength and courage to go forward. My whole former lifetime had been swept away in a blink of time. And what of Lesley, now also faced with this terrible and life changing situation?

Lesley has been my beautiful wife and life partner going on decades. She was there at the local hospital in the beginning and all the way through all of this and more to come. She has become a true hero in the midst of giant and challenging circumstances that presented themselves to her. Lesley was there in the first days when the neurosurgeon came in and described what could be physically done. He outlined a surgery that would be to open the spine and take some parts out and then remove "lesions" pressing on the spine. The outcome was described as bleak, enabling me to walk again but with the possibility of the spine to collapse and perhaps not to heal completely. In hearing this, Lesley began to shake visibly, and become very pale. In that moment I told the neurosurgeon "no", and that I would take whatever next alternative there was. That would be radiation, heavy radiation.

I am not adverse to speaking of such things here, because of the extraordinary "vision" I was blessed with further down the road. I write now from a totally different viewpoint because of this. I am no more my body than the plant across the room. It is the same with all of us. This I learned in the moments still to come in life.

We do indeed live in a "tent of flesh", as Daniel in the Bible described. We are indeed just "dust" in comparison to who we really are that lives within the body, yet it is the only true home we've ever had.

The neurosurgeon came and went an approximate eight or nine times, each time I told him the same basic thing. No surgery, and please look a little closer. There was no need to put out the smoke, but a real need to put out the fire. The spine was perhaps only a result of another area. Graciously, he did hunt further and yes, on his last visit, he did indeed disclose that a group in Hawaii examining CT and MRI imaging as well as his compatriot surgeons had come to a "same" conclusion: That the cancer started elsewhere, the prostate, and had moved up into the spine. I remember him saying, "I don't know where you are getting this wisdom from, but you were correct".

For the next days, I was prepared for radiation. My body was not in a good enough state to withstand the fiery power of the treatments. I was anemic and needed blood and platelet transfusions. It became a situation of wondering what would be the strongest: The patient, the cancer or the cure. I was to have several weeks of daily radiation. The attending crew would routinely gurney me to the radiation room, set me on a rising table, align their "cannon" to aiming marks made on my sternum and circle the "cannon" below the raised table I lay on, then clear the room. I could hear a heavy door being closed as they said," now don't move". A heavy hum was heard as the power of the sun radiated through me. I would often count the seconds while the hum sounded of the blast through me.

The average was thirty seconds as I counted. Then they'd lower me, gurney me back to my room and afterwards I would stare out the window with so many life questions in my mind.

During this time, I often wrote in a small silver notebook in the evenings or late at night when I could not sleep, which was nearly every night. I began to form an idea of regimens that I could do myself that could make a huge difference in the outcome of all. I felt I had to have a personal goal to avoid being tossed around by feelings and simply accepting whatever happened. My own inner voice said it loud and clear: "DEFINE A GOAL". That would become my anchor, the very reason to tie in every action and thought towards a chosen goal. Whatever I could not control outside of me actually had no bearing on what I chose INSIDE of me. It was up to me alone to control my inner abilities and thoughts, feelings and direction. I realized I could CHOOSE, internally, and help to steer the whole ship of my life, body, mind and heart. It was either that or sink in the waves of despair.

My goal became to walk again and heal, to live a new life, to stand up again even after the hardest of blows. I could easily see myself as walking again and being well, and so every time I thought of this I imagined such. Any time it came to me, I imagined and it became a routine to see these goals, within. It became my immoveable goal that I would not accept anything short of it. Two naturally endowed features of anyone towards a single good purpose is the mind and the heart, and indeed you must put your heart into anything worthwhile. The entertaining of negative feelings and thoughts had to go, period. This would take some diligence on my part, but what could be easier than to choose the positive over the negative? It became clear to me that I had recognized the power to choose. In spite of being like boiled spaghetti from the waist down, with next to no feeling, I chose something different to be the outcome. I would choose to walk instead, to rise instead. That's crazy, but it hurt nothing to follow that path. Crazy as it might seem, even as a last and desperate act, I would BELIEVE.

Time progressed through the weeks. Often, I was visited by Dr. Aronson, an oncologist, in cancer care. He and I had hit it off like cake and ice cream from day one. I would ask him if he felt I would walk again, and he would say to me and my over boiled spaghetti legs "I don't know" while wearing a look that said "not likely". I had seen this before from others and it was not a new routine. Yet, in Dr. Aronson's eyes I also saw compassion that was real.

One day near the end of my stay at the cancer center, Dr. Aronson walked in and was talking to me while I surreptitiously showed off my new found activity: After weeks of silently believing, meditating and imagining another outcome, I could wiggle my toes and move my legs.

A tiny bit, but enough that he did a double take and then began to comment on this and poke my feet searching for feeling, and how much, with keen interest. The day before I had noticed to my surprise and astonishment that this had come about. I was now entertaining the impossible. Could this be from the help of imagining? Could this be a revelation towards a new avenue in patient care that DOES hand power over to the patient towards greater end results? Would teaching a patient to imagine and be positive produce a quicker healing and a superior finality?

I had often heard that "the impossible can be done, but takes a little longer", and I was going to continue and find out. I had made a goal to achieve and stuck to a method that seemed to have an influence on getting there. I remembered a well documented story of a man that had cured himself of cancer by daily watching a lot of comedy films, raising his level of joy and laughter and rejecting the negative. My thoughts were to wait before saying anything, and see if others along the way noticed a marked acceleration in my progress, or at least progress in a direction away from the believed paralysis. The last day of radiation I was also shipped off to the rehabilitation hospital in Portland. Behind me I left people of great consideration and care who thought nothing of crossing the border between professional job description and true human compassion.

The "Invisible Tiger" and the gauntlet to kill the beast was, in my mind and that of others, uncertain of outcome at this time. This is when we pray, whether we believe or not, that in our smallness something of greatness would deliver us.

(3)

The Two Lauras'

Lesley and I were separated by a hundred miles and more. Every visit by her was relished, her soft blue eyes and smile were a blessing on my heart and soul. Living in one of the tragedies of life, you quickly find the greatest treasures you had all along. She would light up my spirit by her mere presence. Internally, she was a soothing balm to my heart in all that I faced. Arriving at the rehab unit with next to nothing, she brought some hooded sweatshirts and colored t-shirts, a red plaid pajama bottom. Her Australian accent is calming to anyone, and she is beloved by many. She at first tried to visit several times a week, but I told her that I was concerned about all that travel. Winter was coming in, cold and snowy, and not safe for so much driving. We talked by phone a lot, so she needed not press herself with those very long drives. Once a week would be fine, and her presence as a punctuation of joy all the more appreciated.

While still at the cancer center, Lesley would bring me "fast food" as a welcome change from hospital fare, often with a friend or family in tow. She helped me to have a true sense of not being alone, was an advocate in my life while I was stalled and unable to do much more than be a "professional patient". One of her close friends that visited had brought a sketch pad, which migrated with me to the rehab unit. It became a good way to introduce myself to the staff there by drawing.

Over the first two days, I was introduced to Dr. Benjamin Branch, a man of deeply riveting attention towards his patients. He was well informed about me, a good sense of humor and not stiff in the least bit and very fluid and open in his being, regardless of carrying the responsibility of his large position overall. He also noted the "wigglings" of my feet and legs, and in spite of the assumption so far of paralysis, seemed to view the possibilities. No one, however, in the kindness of their nature, would actually say to me, "you shall not walk again". Unknown to all, I continued my chosen practices of visualization, absolute insistence of a positive nature now being ingrained, and my right to "choose" a better outcome. To heal, to walk, to be well, to defy the odds and entertain the impossible as "do-able", even unto miracles was my choice.

Also in the first two days, I was introduced to the two "Lauras'", Laura Young and Laura Tardie. These two were of the physical and occupational therapy department, and I met them individually at different times. I was very struck by the fact of their intelligence, professionalism, insight bordering on "intuitive" as to the nature of every patient's need in development, their knowledge and very careful handling of so many "lightning struck" individuals harmed by stroke, aneurism, spinal injuries, amputations and more. And, as a final boost, they were beautiful!

Easily, they could step beyond the borders of their professionalism that often dictates to most, "not in my job description", and present the very human compassion and care that is so needed in such a profession.

There is huge frustration being numb and un-working from the waist down. Assisted help to simply get out of a bed and into a wheelchair and back was personally humbling, and nothing I had ever dreamed of happening to me. True to my goal, I changed the negative and self depreciated thoughts and feelings to something higher, a challenge and one of the steps on my way to "the goal".

Laura "T" helped me with the finer points of "how to do" these tasks, moving to seats, the commode, the wheelchair and on. However, I was scolded on many an occasion by the nursing staff to not get out of the bed without their presence. I could be seen as stubborn and too ambitious, but internally was simply heeding the call towards "the goal". But I promised I would call for assistance or observation.

Only days there, Laura Young escorted me down to the physical therapy area and put me before a set of parallel bars, locking my wheelchair into place.

"O.K., I want you to grab the parallel bars, and stand up", Laura said.

Sheesh! For a moment I thought she said she wanted me to stand up! Then I realized she DID want me to stand up. My mind went suddenly blank, then raced like crazy. "My goodness! How am I going to do THAT"!

"Just use your upper body strength and use the bars to lift yourself up. You can do it", Laura said. "I'm right here and I will help you", she added.

I felt I was faced with the impossible, faced with finding out the truth of the matter, even discovering that I truly would'nt walk again. I was scared, but somehow trusted in Laura with all my belief, that if she felt I could DO this and BELIEVED it, chances were that it COULD be done. I strove with what strengths I had and pulled myself forward…and up. "Lock your knees when you get up", Laura said.

Suddenly, I was standing. I was terrified and in ecstasy, both at the same moment. I felt like I was a mile high. I was feeling like a fledgling that had leaped from the nest, wondering if I had grown enough feathers to fly, or maybe would bounce twice in landing hard. After weeks and weeks of sitting or in a bed, I was STANDING! My landing into the wheelchair was uneventful but internally I was high as a kite. "How we believe is where we are going to", flashed through my mind.

I imagine that outside of me anyone viewing this simply saw one man struggling to do what was taken for granted by almost everyone. No big deal, but to the "lightning struck" individual it was a task, a challenge and an accomplishment of very deep importance. I recognized that the common person would have no real understanding of "being there" and facing the labor of regaining a lost connection to one's body. I still had trouble believing that this had actually happened to me, and it caused a strange shift in my mind. I had both subjective and objective viewpoints going on. I was personally in the midst of a struggle that was happening to me, and somehow I also saw it from the standpoint of observing the reactions of my body, my mind and my feelings from a "removed" position. It was like "being" the person going through the actions and "being" a person outside and watching the actions in another individual. A real moment of ZEN, anyone?

What was this that I was seeing? Or should I say, "seeing" as an internal realization? On a rehab unit full of "lightning struck" individuals, it was clear that unless you were one you had no idea of the experience, no conception of the struggle that was completely internal in it's nature. Broken connections had to be rejoined, if they could, and to identify too much with the body in trouble would certainly cause great mental and emotional grief, depression and despair. Yes, and often, I saw a lethargic and hollow look in the eyes those around me. Better to be ZEN about it and have the "dual" viewpoint. I had recognized, now, that I WAS a "lightning struck" individual. I also realized that but for my own broken connection, internally I was whole.

In spite of it being a tragedy, it also presented itself as being one of the greatest learning experiences one can have. A "kinship" with those who have struggled, or are struggling, could only light one's compassion for others and even enhance one's inner strength and knowledge on a higher scale.

I'm not certain that many of those around me recognized they lived and had "being" in a higher state than just the body, but my ZEN moment revealed that they were doing something that was "above the average common individual" and were learning something the common individual would never, ever know. The idea and learning of mind over matter.

Take a pen and write your name on a piece of paper. You have just done mind over matter. If you can tell your body what to do, well then you can tell your body what to do! You intended something mentally and sent it down into the physical. The "lightning struck" individual has a disconnect in nerves that is physical, and it is clearly possible to "grow" new connections by thinking towards them. My GOAL was all about this. Crazy? You bet, but there is ample evidence that this is a scientifically proven reality. Again, if you think you can do something, chances are that you can.

Two days after first standing freeform in the parallel bars, Laura Young brought me back to them. A new contraption was introduced where I was strapped in to an overhead electrical lift. It had the advantage of a structure on the ceiling that allowed you to be supported and also walk over half the PT room in any direction. "O.K., I am going to lift you up out of your wheelchair, so just go with it and lift yourself up", said Laura.

Another therapist walked into the room and asked her a question as she was pushing the "up" button on a wire lead to the motor, momentarily distracting her as I lifted myself up. I stood and the straps became supportive…and then continued on and lifted me clear off the floor, dangling, swinging and twirling. Also at that moment, three quarter of a dozen people turned and watched, then burst into laughter as I swayed and twirled above the floor. Laura suddenly turned around and saw this spectacle, embarrassed but laughing also, and stopped the motor.

"I feel like Tinkerbell! I'm flying!", I said, swaying. Then she let me down to touch the floor, saying, "sorry, sorry", while laughing. We all got a good chuckle and christened the machine "Tinkerbell", which stuck from that day forth.

And on that day I took my first two steps. Rough, unadorned and sloppy, but I took my first two steps. I felt like I was riding a horse that was impaired, the body the horse and I the rider.

The next day I was again strapped into "Tinkerbell", raised and then took twenty sloppy steps forward in the parallel bars, and then eighteen back. Wow.

And the day after that I took eighty steps, down and back several times in "Tinkerbell". My legs and feet were roughly moving but went through the actions. This was very promising in spite of inwardly seeing the hard climb ahead of me.

I was told that I could be released about ten days ahead and after Christmas. Every single day until then I was exercising and spent time with "Tinkerbell", Laura "Y" and Laura "T".

Laura "T", as an occupational therapist, prepared me in the mean time to be able to function at home in a wheelchair, as actual free form walking in a walker or later in a cane was still a real distance off. Lesley had acquired a wheelchair for free, which was exellent on her part because they were so expensive. Physical therapists to come to our home were to be arranged, and to help me further if the body would allow.

Although it was not openly said, it was clear that I had made some progress, but not enough to be convincing of how far I would progress. It may be that later I could walk to some degree, but I could still become wheelchair bound for the most part.

Perhaps I should have stayed longer at the rehab center but I had had real concerns for Lesley while I was so far away and in no state to be of much help. Winter was starting in earnest and made travel even harder and more grueling, and with two dogs, a cat, a woodstove and snow piling up, plus working, she was more than hard pressed, to say the least, in keeping home running. She also handled paperworks and the people needed to help with the finances of this terrible event. In the midst of stacked difficulties, a hero came forth to help her in her very real problems and hard moments. Our neighbor, Don Pendleton, was a true saving grace, and would clear snow, let the dogs in and out, stacked our wood and brought in kindling in large bags, fed the woodstove and turned on the lights when darkness fell. This is a man of heart who called me often at the rehab unit and helped in many ways. I can't imagine how we could have gotten through without all his help, and he proved to me that there are many good people in the world.

On the twenty eighth of December, goodbyes were said to the two Laura's, the good Dr. Branch, and I went home, assisted into the house by kindly neighbors, including Don.

Two days later on the first of January, incredibly, another disaster struck as large as the first. The stage was set for miracles.

(4)

Ashes, Ashes, All Fall Down

And on the third day, I descended into the Valley of the Shadow. It was as falling asleep and not remembering the moment, and it was as dreaming and you don't know reality the way you had before. Like a sinking ship, one entered limbo, a dark place of neither life nor death. The body overcome, the embers of consciousness dissipated like ashes on the wind by the onslaught of an invasion.

The temple of the body lay on the bed and the spirit and soul withdrew into a nothingness. The soldiers of the tent of flesh fought in vain and were being overcome by the mass of the dark army, bent on a slow and meticulous murder. Like a bird stricken in the heavens, a downward spiral into deeper and deeper darkness was entered, the temple consigned to destruction.

Lesley, on a whim and urge, left work at the hospital to spend lunch time at home. All seemed normal in arriving until she called out and got no response. And in finding me she instantly knew that there was more than "something wrong". The ambulance called for, the flurry of activity to the hospital, the placement in the intensive care unit and the recognition of the killer influenza "A", another type of influenza and bacterial pneumonia was like being in New Jersey rush hour traffic. The prospects did not look good and very much leaned towards the negative. A fifty, fifty chance of survival existed, and worried doctors came and went.

Gasping for air and brought through x-ray, it was clear that my lungs were filling and I was drowning. An attempt to help me with a breathing mask made my body react automatically to the claustrophobic unit by tearing it off, and the next action by the staff was to induce coma by drugs. The body relaxed, unable to fight off those attempting to assist me in staying alive. Now the body was just as the one who lived in it, subdued and in coma.

Although the body and temple had fought on, the conscious one who lived within had departed long before into oblivion and beyond. The "I" was missing since lying down on the bed at home.

From that point forth there was no recognition by the "I" of the events in the physical world that were happening.

For two days the body and worldly semblance of "Dennis" stayed stable but slipping, much to the worry and building fear of the medical staff and Lesley. The falling bird was going deeper into a downward spiral, and life ebbing away. A decision was reached to ship the failing shell by airflight to a facility in Portland where stabilization and retrieval might be possible. A friend who was present spoke to Lesley, both of them distraught over the frightening recognition that all were talking of a final demise. And just quickly, the friend caught a glimpse of a shaking of the head from the "temple", symbolically saying, "No, I shall not die!".

From beneath the intubations and paraphernalia, the spirit, soul, heart and mind had momentarily cried out in a gesture, then was gone again into oblivion.

Arriving in Portland, all recognized the serious situation that continued it's course slowly downwards, and time ticked on through days in the ICU. A week and the body began to puff up like a sausage in becoming more septic. The deciding moments were around the eighth and ninth day, and all believed the time was at hand. Lesley was there, renting a hotel room and living in dire grief. She lit candles and prayed to the one God we all know in spite of religious belief. Family and friends came and sat in the vigil. There seemed to be no way out but down. The temple was to fall.

At the ICU on a following day, Lesley took a break and stepped away and into another room. There she happened to bump into a doctor that later she described as "utterly beautiful", a good looking and gorgeous man. She described it as a beauty that bordered on going beyond human form. He introduced himself, stating his name and commenting that he was Greek and then offered, "but you can call me Nick". A conversation ensued and Lesley, being a psychiatric nurse, suggested that an anti-anxiety drug might help the situation with "Dennis", seeing as the point had been reached where nothing was helping. She felt this could at least ease the state of being and the inner distress. The Doctor listened, responded by the action of doing so, recognizing that this could be helpful in the face of things, and not harmful at all.

Weeks from that moment, this subject would be brought up, not as a subtle point of jealousy, but as an unusual circumstantial moment. That the Doctor was Greek was what became of clear interest. That the name "Dennis" is originally Greek and so also is the Phoenix added to the coincidences and oddly fit into what was to happen next. Unknown to all and at the instant of death, my Journey was traveled under guidance, away from the world that we know. And but for moments the last spark of life succumbed to darkness, as that last ember finally failed. All floated far away like ashes in a breeze on a distant and etheric landscape of changing form.

Dennis was no more. He died.

Then somehow, a slight breeze of the breath of life returned and began to raise the broken bird's spiral out of the dark places it had drifted, lost. But for a moment it had been snuffed as the light of a candle. Out of the ash, one tiny ember somehow revived and held in the void and blackness. It caught, glowed and grew.

The Doctor's assistance seemed to be of help, and over the next twenty four hours or more, a reversal of the broken bird's downward spiral of flight into death became noticed.

It was feared that "Dennis" would drown in the ventilator, and it had to come off, and so it was removed. Like a portend to take advantage of, slowly rising signs signaled that the moment had arrived, hopes confirmed, prayers answered, life renewed, the temple saved, and all waited for the "I" that was missing to come forth. It took nearly a week more.

(5)

Netherworlds

And I suddenly found myself in a dark landscape with even darker skies. It had a feeling of being more real than in so-called normal life. Other people numbering several dozen and more were present and the immediate land was angled down towards a body of water. A voice spoke out of somewhere and told me that I was at the River Styx. I could not tell if the voice had come from without or within. All of this was shocking because it was more than real. It was as if my whole life had been as a dream and now I had awakened in a place I did not wish to be. Everything was in tones of grey, brown black and shadows. The people mulled about as I looked at the shore, the oily water with small and greasy ripples and a thick fog out on the river. There was a slight amber glow directly out and in the fog. The sky was black. The glow in the fog was curious, as it seemed to be very slowly becoming brighter.

Suddenly I heard a man shout out loudly, and all the surrounding people turned towards him to listen. He was but ten feet away from me, addressing the crowd and then turning and looking at me. He loudly said, "Who will give this man a coin, that he may pass over?". One did not cross over the River Styx unless they paid the Boatman a coin, and I had none. All looked at me, and then individually turned away, unwilling to give a simple coin.

In that darkened place and in my consternation I was stricken even further that no one would help me at all. And there was a fear in the air about this giving of a coin. In the air itself could be felt and reasoned why no coin would be given. It felt as though to do such would be against the will of GOD, and the curse and wrath of Him would fall instantly upon the one who gave the coin. It clearly told me that no one wanted me to cross to Hades, where both heaven and hell and everything in between existed, and where one received their fair and eternal reward for the life one had lived.

I did'nt know what to do, did'nt know where to go or what to think as despair and uncertainty washed through me.

Through the thick fog, the source of the glow finally revealed itself as the coming "Boatman". At this point I could clearly see his large and floppy hat, the bulging eyes and the flaming torches on the sides of the boat.

At that instance of gazing on the fearful scene, and out of nowhere, a brilliant light came on to my right side and arm's length away. It was so impossibly bright that the whole crowd of people fell back and turned away, shielding their eyes from the utter brilliance. I, too, had turned away from the light, but then was taken by curiosity and turned back to look at the brilliance. As I squinted into the flood of rays, again I heard a voice from somewhere, say, "This is your Guardian, full of light, come to take you back to the land of the living".

Squinting, I looked into the brilliance and saw a being, an entity, a creature of the light: My Guardian. I was surprised to see it looking straight up, then turning to look directly at me as I got used to staring into the brightness. A shape of the head and eyes of blue and distinctly feminine, and robed in glorious rays and light. Here stood a softness, a sweetness, a love and a height of power that could not be rivaled. A Living Will of God. The atmosphere was filled with thoughts, ideas, knowledge and concepts of such simplicity and beauty, and seemed to flow into me and through me and around me. It had never in my life been so clear as this moment where I could actually feel and know the love of our Guardian for us, and how it is utterly a sacred duty to them that they protect us. And it is far more than our body or ways of life that is protected, but rather our core, our being and spirit. The greater part of us.

The Guardian turned and started to walk away, and then stopped, turned and looked at me again, with a look that said, "Well, are you coming?". I followed up the bank and away from the River Styx and went wherever the Guardian walked. Often she would turn to me and tell me the timeless phrase, "Do not fear". I heard this many times. The whole landscape was lit up around us as we walked and the sky turned from black to purple, and the vague patches of clouds could be seen. The atmosphere around the Guardian continued to be full of thoughts, ideas, knowledge and concepts, and continued to flow even through me. As I walked I realized that I was picking something up from it, and would be bringing it back with me. I would not be returning empty handed. The sky had turned from purple to deep blue and showed amber clouds catching the first lights of the day coming. I continued to follow the Guardian as the sky turned true blue and the clouds were white. Even though the sun was to rise, the brilliance of the Guardian was far beyond the sun in intensity, and when the moment of sunrise came, I turned and saw the first rays of the new morning so glorious.

I was suddenly sitting in a bed with tubes up my nose and a tray in my lap. Stunned, I reached up with my left arm to feel something on my face, tubes inserted into my nose. They were short and I recognized them as oxygen tubes, I felt the bands around my ears holding them in place. WHAT THE HECK IS GOING ON?? Where am I? How did I get here? Why is it hard to raise my arm?....

and then looking at my left arm I was appalled to see what resembled a stick with rubber bands hanging off of it, and so weak I could not raise it above my chest. I was thin as a broom!

I was in a hospital room that I did not remember being brought to, with a food tray having been given that I did not remember arriving. But I DID remember the most recent event of life being walking with an Angel. I saw it, was witness to it, and knew it to be the truth. There was no way of explaining just yet that there were other levels of reality than this, the physical. From the background of my mind, other memories of many places were also coming forth in things that I had seen while "gone". And yes, I knew I had been "gone" and elsewhere, like I had been a cosmic traveler on a tour of an inner and far bigger universe than we recognize.

At first, I just sat there, completely flabbergasted, and yet there was also a sense of utter joy, and a recognition that a new and great insight into life had been given to me.

There were voices just outside the room. Two people were talking about someone who had been ill to the point of death and flown in to the hospital, and that it was expected that he was going to die. I recognized from the conversation it was two doctors talking and I thought to myself, "wow! That poor guy!".

As the conversation continued, they then mentioned the person's name: "Dennis".

Suddenly realizing that you had almost died, or did, is quite a stunner. And something was now learned and understood that was so far different than the way we have believed of life, death and all in between. As the body and temple fell to the very doors of death, a very large group of events and experiences were still cognizant, clear, linear and fully remembered. One could call them "dreams" or visions, but how can this be if the body is the seat of all memory, thought, emotion and consciousness? The body was a crashed wreck at the time, hardly able to produce coherent stories.

Out of body experiences are not new. It was clear and irrevocably believed that I had experienced such. I was going to have to carefully filter through every memory and judiciously decide what was fantasy and what was "vision".

But there I sat after being delivered by my Guardian, a divine act letting me know the Heavens were truly there. No, I had not come out of wherever I had been "empty handed", and the thoughts and concepts brought forth were very powerful concepts and understandings. I understood, by the simple and pure experience, that we cannot "see" our Guardian in life because we are at the wrong level, or frequency, of consciousness to "see". At the gates of death, our frequency is changed and closer to the universal order of all things.

I was sitting in a bed in recovery from a lethal illness, still unable to walk, having lost forty pounds over sixteen days, yet was never so at peace within myself. I had undergone a journey of incredible depth that was certainly going to be hard to explain, culminating in a meeting with the Divine. I had "seen" beyond our small and common human form and found a greatness in us, buried and waiting to awaken. The entire universe was alive and constantly in the state of creation, and there was no such thing as death, just transformation, and we do not travel alone.

Do not fear.

Several days later in the recovery room, I was visited by Dr. Aronson whom I had hit it off with like "cake and ice cream" at the cancer center. He said, "Well, you made it through. It's no surprise, though, that you picked up something".

"Any cancer patient who has been through treatment has a very low immunity afterwards", he said.

"Does that mean I'll pick up something else?", I asked.

"You? No", Dr. Aronson said. "Heck, if you made it through this, you'll probably never be sick again! You'll probably die of old age, knowing you! And they'll probably boil you down and make you into a cure-all for everything!" We laughed at this pretty good.

But having such a setback meant that I would have to gain back weight and strength as well as learn to walk again. That meant a return to a rehabilitation center and almost starting from scratch.

How much does one have to go through in life? Perhaps enough to learn the incredible power of the living, human spirit that is fully attached to God, although we don't realize it. We come into life with "cosmic amnesia".

Gaining a wheelchair to get out and exercise on the floors of the recovery area, several weeks passed in the uncertainty of where I would go next. I still needed help in simply going from bed to chair, or the reverse. Lesley and I talked on the phone quite often, and that was discussed. And I knew something that I did'nt know before: The universe and existence has a real tendency to hear us and provide what is necessary in our journey. Everything arrives "on time" and yet depends on our attitude towards the positive or the negative. We can miss the greatest of gifts by refusing to have faith, or we can patiently wait for the good to come. I was rewarded for my believing, as those doors opened and I was accepted back to the original rehabilitation unit, the one with the fiery "Phoenix" inlaid on the hall floor. I saw it as more than quite a coincidence. Death and resurrection. Although I had burst into flames, fallen and become ashes, I was being reborn.

I was become "the Phoenix". I had taken an unexpected sideline journey that was proving to not be an immense, personal catastrophe, but a gigantic blessing of a higher nature. I was going to put to the test and LIVE the very things I had "seen", learned and been given in that "sideline journey".

I was transferred to the rehab unit and was there for several days when the staff psychologist came for a visit. Dr. Ireland is a tall, bright eyed gentleman with a distinct leaning towards really understanding his patients. His is not a job, but a dedication to the inner welfare of the "lightning struck" individual. I had met him before in my last visit to the unit, and I'm sure he breathed easier for finding a sound and cheerful patient in me.

So, I'm sure that he was deeply interested in my state of being after such a harrowing interlude such as triple pneumonia and coma. He and I had seen "eye to eye and above the water" on all occasions in the past, and it was he who had spoken of the art and technique of "positive visualization" in our good conversations of this subject. This man was NO dummy and well versed and experienced in many things seen in patients. I have been around the "cosmic block" a few times, and I recognized this same depth in him.

"So, is there anything you'd like to talk about in your experience on the ICU? Any thoughts or feelings you have?", he asked me.

"As a matter of fact, yes. I'd like to tell you about something I saw while in coma", I said, and then told him of the vision, the River Styx, the Guardian and the brilliant light.

When I was through, I had the power of conviction written in my eyes that something extraordinary had taken place. What Dr. Ireland said next took me by complete surprise, although anything he or anyone else would have said would not have made a "jot" of difference in my total conviction. Although paraphrased, this is what he conveyed:

"I have seen many people come and go. Most get better and leave. Then sometimes some come and do not leave, but die, and that is that. Then, every now and then but rarely, some come that have reached the doors of death and then return with such stories as yours. It is a "Near Death Experience", and this is what I believe you have had".

At that moment and in hearing this from Dr. Ireland, I KNEW he understood on a level that was far deeper than commonly understood, and gained from me a huge appreciation for this man's clear depth, comprehension and knowledge.

These things DO happen. Yet there were other things that I had seen that needed to be processed, digested and contemplated in order to recognize the meanings in them. Much spoke of humanity's need to grow and have a larger comprehension of our real value as human beings, especially to each other, rather than the shallow and "3-D horizontal only" assumption of being cut-off individuals in a giant universe. In 3D, it's big enough, but by adding the knowledge of layers of existence it becomes incomprehensibly huge. But so does our potential, individually and collectively.

So, how can a series of "dreams" culminate in a vision of an angel, punctuated in the end with sudden and total consciousness in a hospital bed?

What you believe is where you are going to. Should you be shown something higher by experience, you have the great opportunity to embrace something higher. I was going to do something that would be considered impossible, and that was a new belief that it was possible.

I was going to walk again. What I believed is where I was going to. If you believe you can do something, chances are very great that you can. But you must believe.

In the mean time, I was going to sort out a few dreams and visions while "rehabing". Ample time existed between the hub-bub of meeting with physical or occupational therapy groups, and those moments were going to become my laboratory. Otherwise, time would be wasted on watching a multitude of vapid television stations in bed. I would rather turn inward, open up the memory and review anything I could bring up "in mind". A rather interesting and novel idea is to become your own laboratory and sort through the scraps and chips and chunks that were there. And a quick review showed that a large body of memory from my journey ran in linear story lines, some even like documentaries. They could almost be put in order, and had so much realistic and applicable content that it clashed with my "idea" as to what a dream was supposed to be.

I was also fully aware that coma and drugs can produce a psychotic mindset, hallucinatory and distorted to the point that a lucid and cognizant consciousness could quickly and easily recognize those things. So my time would be spent filtering out stray and nonsense things while also seeing more clearly the dreams or visions that had portend, substance, meaning.

The vision of the Guardian was a thing set in stone and permanently accepted. The Greek motif was baffling, though. I have no Greek lineage or influence that I can think of at all.

Meanwhile, appointments were set to begin with the therapy groups, and my activity in a wheel chair commenced out in the halls of the rehab unit. It was actually good to see some familiar faces again, rather than a new batch of strangers to learn about. I

did get a warm welcome, the staff aware of the tremendous battle I had just gone through simply to be alive. In rolling through the now farmiliar hallways in a wheelchair, the symbol of the Phoenix emblazoned into the floor took on a much deeper and more significant meaning. I had become as the Phoenix.

I realized this as a story of "everyone", not simply me. Alone, I would certainly not have lived to complete the course. Even the Guardian, as the will of God, helped me back to this land of the living, yet I was sent back not knowing what it was that I must complete. Life is life, and as such is a mystery. And yet the Phoenix knows some of the mystery of life itself, by clear experience. So do I.

(6)

The Ascent

The staff still would not let me get in and out of the wheelchair, or bed, and now for obvious reasons. I had lost weight and also muscle strength in my stay at the ICU. What was next at the rehab unit was to regain the strength lost as well as work on reconnecting to some very lethargic legs and torso.

My viewpoint of my current physical state, as opposed to the viewpoint of those around me, was markedly different and this was obvious to me. It was another "Zen" moment where interior-wise self-knowledge could not be conveyed to those in the exterior. I could sense very clearly, and determined with inner conviction, that the state of being wheelchair bound was not permanent.

From the exterior, I looked like an overly cheerful and positive individual that was not yet aware of being permanently paralyzed.

From the interior, I saw a construction project that could certainly be done and accomplished by the now understood inner power that we all posess.

Enter again the two "Lauras'" and the illustrious Dr. Branch into the rise from the ashes. With Laura "T", I began routine upper body strengthening on the weight machine, and "classes" in a group where aerobic rubber bands were used. In my first visit to this class, I entered the room in my wheelchair to discover a plastic skeleton hung on a tall pole in the corner. It was adorned with a silver "tiara" on its head and a Hawaiian "lai" around it's neck, a sight to behold towards humor.

Since coming out of coma in what had been to me an instantaneous "flash", I had recognized and carried forth a sense that a "something" like a "presence" was always there, and that I had not returned "empty handed". A change of mind and stature within was what I carried with me, and shared willingly with all.

It was a glow that silently said, "do not fear" and reinforced the whole idea of being of good cheer towards everything, no matter what. And there before me in this rubber band group I saw the "lightning struck" of various ages and walks of life. People harmed and feeling low in themselves for what had become….and who they thought they had become. "What you believe is where you are going to" rings true in every moment of our lives, and in spite of my state of affairs, no one and nothing had the right to dictate how I would feel internally. I would CHOOSE what I felt within. And this is infectious, to be of positive nature in the midst of others so hard hit by life. My glowing ember could be fanned into a bright and uplifting thing, a light for others that helped them transfer from a habit of self inflicted sorrow to something far more powerful.

Hope.

But hope needs a reason to hope, and what better than an individual that shines in spite of their own situation. That light is a presence that touches everything. "The kingdom of Heaven is within", and that is the very core of our existence, although we have mostly forgotten. In the group, we ALL began to improve in small increments that became obvious in a short weeks time. Yes, I smiled at them, smiled with them, cajoled them, laughed with them, strived with them.

Laura "T" also began to teach me in the occupational area set up as a kitchen. She began to teach me how to rise up out of my wheelchair and stand at a counter. In freeform, I could'nt stand for long even holding on to the counter, needing more development, but that would come in time. Shortly after, in one of Lesley's visits, Laura "T" escorted us to the kitchen and described my task, which was to stand at the counter, unassisted by holding on, and make a peanut butter sandwich.

"Yaah! That's too high! I don't know!", I said, but encouraged by Laura "T", and with Lesley watching, I rose, made the sandwich and then sat back down. I was not the only one stunned by that progress. In fact, all three of us were quite amazed, and this set the bar higher for accomplishment, an accomplishment that originally was not expected at all by any. Lesley was amazed and hope sprang up like the sun. I continued to "imagine" walking. I truly believed it was just down the road a little ways. Miracles were brewing.

What was this? I had suddenly started having massive improvements in what was shortly before unresponsive limbs. You can't imagine how I felt. And in fact, we were ALL watching something of a miracle occur.

During the week, Laura Young fetched me and began to daily strap me in to the support of "Tinkerbell", where I would rise, without flying this time, and walk the length and back of the parallel bars many times. There came a time, then, where she had me walk right out of the bars and into the open. After a few of these tentative excursions, I was walking in a "walker" about the room with "Tinkerbell". Laura "Y's" patience, guidance, support and encouragement were so very important in this time. She was one of the important keys, as Laura "T" also was, in handing my life back to me. This was a trip! What an excitement! Although supported by "Tinkerbell" and a walker, I was walking.

Not really great, but walking. Mr.Spaghetti legs was walking.

This was not really expected by anyone, originally, but with this came an astonished interest on the part of the doctors and also others. Clearly, this was surprising and caught much attention and enthusiasm. Some even came forth privately and asked, "what are you doing that is making this so?". I would quickly explain "envisioning" and belief upwards of one hundred percent. We can choose to trade off old beliefs for something greater than what we had believed. We can choose to cast out all negative assumptions and thoughts, even feelings. And in doing this we must also constantly be on guard against any thought, any feeling or even action tainted by the negative. It is our right to choose how we feel and think, and it is in our capacity to do so. And in choosing this, we are connected to something far greater than the darkness we have unwittingly accepted. It is a path towards light, as opposed to our habitual entertaining of the dark and negative.

Dr. Ireland and I enjoyed some very open and wonderful conversations about "visualization" and also our amazing and strange connection to something "above us" that we occasionally tap into. Something of a divine nature has an intermittent appearance in our lives from "within". That Dr. Ireland broached these subject areas was welcome to me, as I always had had a leaning of interest in our inner areas. The conscious and subconscious, the super-conscious areas and our cognizance as an individual while also being part of the whole. I would have loved to talk to this man for several hours or more. He is a very, very smart cookie, as they say, and very dedicated to his work.

Dr. Branch also made weekly visits and sometimes more. Of course I delighted in his presence and conversation also. Our conversations would always start with the basics of "Hey! How's your gizzard working?" and such pertinent physiological mechanisms involved in one's current health. But quickly we would find ourselves talking of much more exotic knowledge, such as acupuncture, the growth of neurons, the importance of the heel of the foot in creating blood cells, and many other subjects. He also recognized something quite unusual and uplifting was occurring with my development.

Something totally unexpected was now happening, much in the positive and more than promising. It was, in fact, delivering.

Over seventy percent of the human population believes in angels, and that is another fact. Again, since awakening in the ICU, I knew I did not come out "empty handed", and often sensed the feel of "another presence" with me. Often also, I have had other people try to tell me that they really DID see an angel, as if I would not believe their story. I would offer a bet, here, that some of the readers will be nodding their head at these comments.

The neuro- class was a gathering, again, of the "lightning struck", and often I came in with Laura "Y" to some fairly somber faces. This could always be changed, though, simply by waiting for a moment that could be used towards some humor. Then I could show them that I, too, was "lightning struck". Things that they could do and I could not were pointed out, and that my hope was someday to be able to do such. But the joy and brightness of the living flame within me showed that a cheerful stature did'nt depend on being "normal" in the ordinary sense of the word, but on the choosing of brightness within, rather than the darkness without. The class was about movement and stretching, reaching and standing and then sitting, all towards awakening the memory of the body of such things. Reconnecting the response of old nerves and prompting new nerves and muscles into action. And after this class, there would be some individuals that could walk and would be escorted out of the room to the nearby hall, circling back and coming in through another doorway in the room, and the class would be over. I would tell myself silently that someday I, too, would walk that route, and christened it, "the Walk Around the Block" club. I could now stand, and with the aid of "Tinkerbell" had reached a very close proximity to that club, the "Walk Around the Block".

Days later, Laura "Y" brought me down to the physical therapy room. She parked and locked my wheelchair. Then, Laura "Y" said,

"Stand up". I did, but immediately started to look for something to grab on to: A walker, a table or chair or anything.

"What am I supposed to hold on to?". I asked.

"You're not. WALK", she said. "I've got your arm and you're safe". Tentatively, staggeringly, like a toddler, I walked across the room and then with guided turning, I walked back across the room to the wheelchair and sat down. All that time I was somewhere between uncertainty and sheer joy.

Praises came forth from Laura "Y" as I sat in utter astonishment of what I had just done. I had just walked! I had really just walked!

A tendency of my right knee to become unlocked and buckle was noted, and arrangements were made to fit my legs with braces designed to keep this from happening. News of walking spread to the medical personnel, and it could be felt in the air that this was an amazing and exciting thing. This is the type of happenstance that lights up and raises all of those who have been part of the immense struggle of an individual. And in this case an impossibility was coming about. Very clearly, these people are importantly part of a whole and inclusive story. You can also imagine how I felt after so much had come to pass and even stood in the way of the "goal" I had set for myself. So, "what you believe is where you are going to" has to be said again.

In the midst of this excitement, other things were also being explored pertaining to the many dreams, or visions, that came before the last and final vision at the River Styx. In my room, especially in the evening and at night, was the laboratory I reviewed these "dreams" or visions from while in coma. It should be understood that the near death experience is not all flowers and butterflies and happy, happy. In truth, it is a gauntlet of the spirit, soul and heart, and one comes through it with an entirely changed view. Along with a greater hope than before, I found it much easier to consider, care and even love people. I felt like I had keys to the "Kingdom", yet understood that the world in itself might not understand the absolute reality of other levels, that we can be unbreakable as well as fragile and crush-able at the same time, that we were eternal while being mortal, spirit while being flesh.

LABORATORY 1

It is a valid point to consider that one's consciousness may very well not be a product of the body and nervous system, and that function of the mind may also be "removed" to a certain degree.

I think this is really "old hat" because this has come up over and over again for thousands of years when it comes to death or dying, or to the deceased returning to help us in moments of dire times and need. There are countless stories of their visitation to us on or after departing this land of the flesh, as in death. They are "seen" as still alive when they come, even though the body thought to produce consciousness is gone. So now we have the deceased, as well as those who have had a near death experience, illustrating that clearly the consciousness is above the physical by surviving it's demise. I am leading you, here, by writing what I know. Others also "know" this as part of the result of a near death experience.

There are also the stories and legends of what is termed the "Astral body", or star body, a second body that is said to exist in us on a higher scale or level of frequency. It has been often said that this is the body we inherit at death, and it is said that some have learned to "remove" this body from the physical one and clearly be conscious in it while they perceive and explore elsewhere, but return they must. Patients often have had pain, itching and sensations of touch on missing amputated legs or arms, and it suggests the existence of this other body. Even though it may be something of the imagination, the imagination is certainly part of the mind and it's content, and the mind is real. In dreams we can smell, see, hear, touch, taste. Is this happening because we are "remembering" those senses? And then if so, why do many report of being able to "fly" in a dream, in spite of physically never having flown before?

The very basic difference between a dream and a vision is found by applying simple, common sense observation. Dreams can look real, but are disjointed, erratic and meaningless. I've even had "dreams" during my waking hours, called "daydreams", and I do not mistake them for the more inspired "visions" that hold content and higher thinking. Visions are fluid, sequential, linear as in a storyline and point to a meaning that needs no interpretations.

Having or being in a vision connotes the five senses and their activity in a higher state and scale, comprised of themselves collectively in a "body".

It may seem to many like I have driven myself "out on a limb" to suggest that we have another body, but there is also many who have had "out of body experiences" and also near death experiences that compound the reality. It would do a great service to humanity if we were made aware that we have a built-in stepping stone towards the heavens in this understanding, and dissipate many fears of what we call death. In total, there are far more voices and writings that speak of such a reality than against it. I believe that it is the other body that is our inheritance and the next temple of our consciousness that is so surely protected by such as one's Guardian, as well as the body, mind and heart we live in while in the 3D horizontal world.

This being said, understanding the dreams and visions becomes much easier, as even "slides in time" can occur either forward or back. The Heavens have a different time, structure, feel and "air" that often defies description.

I sometimes have told the story of the Guardian to a complete stranger, one time to a woman who only afterwards told me that she had had a near death experience but had had much trouble rectifying what she thought of as conflicting images. She felt that she could tell no one because of this, until she heard my vision and description of the light with the darkness, as with being at the River Styx. In telling her, there was a moment when her eyes suddenly took on a sparkle of recognition, and I stopped momentarily to say, "and you know why I am telling you this, don't you?" and she agreed because many things that she could not rectify suddenly fell into place, to her great relief.

And so the visions have their meaning, not simply to me, but to others that may hear. They are plain and straight forward and in need of no interpretation.

With this I go forward.

(7)

Like Flying

The braces were form fitted to my legs and soles. Being a thin but stiff plastic, they were to go inside a shoe. For the moment, we tore out the lining of a pair of sneakers so they would fit. But they were hard to get on and off, and so Laura "T" volunteered to take me to a local chain store and find a larger pair. God bless her soul.

Arriving and going through cheap shoes, seeking an appropriate larger pair for "planned obsolescence", the only pair besides a fluorescent orange twosome was a pair that were the spitting image of "Florida retirement" sneakers. Perfect! White as a sun drenched sheet and large enough to hold twenty cups of tea, we bought the good humored shoes and returned. In arriving, I was wearing the "Florida retirement shoes", which caused smiles, chuckles and joy in the face that I was now a miraculous, white shoe'd marvel able to walk. In the physical therapy room, I did a few daily cruises in my new "foot limousines" and in a walker. "Tinkerbell" was now behind me, but I remember those days fondly because of all the help and care put forth from Laura "T" and Laura "Y".

Laura "T" taught me how to get up from the floor, in the advent of maybe falling, rising from level to level and arriving at sitting and then to walker or wheelchair. But the wheelchair and it's days were also doomed not far in the future. In free time during the day, I would go on the public internet available to us and found some cane handles in the head of a bird and of brass. I was already planning to go to a cane while fighting to get out of the wheelchair permanently. I would hand-make the cane when arriving home with the bird-head brass handle.

Although in braces and with a walker, I felt like I was flying when in the physical therapy room, although I did not walk far.

Then came the day in the rubber room, doing exercises with the group and rubber bands. Laura "T" told me that I had to stay after class. At first I thought I might have done something wrong. She brought me out into the hall pulling a wheeled chair and said to me, "I am going to tie myself to the wheelchair and sit on this chair with wheels. I want to see how far you can pull me down the hall. You game?"

"Yaah! YOU BET!". I said, and feeling like Ben Hur and his horses, off we went. Puffing and grunting I made it down half the hall, which is quite a stretch that proved my upper body strength, and strength in general, was returning.

"OK. How far back can you make it?"

"I guess we'll find out!", I said and proceeded to grunt and groan about two thirds the length we came before giving up the game. Both of us felt it was great good fun, and in the days ahead she mentioned this to Dr. Branch, who exclaimed, "When's it MY turn!" and he meant it!

Several more days went by and Laura "T" came to get me at my room. As we passed by the nurse's station, Dr. Branch spotted us and jumped up hauling a wheeled chair with him, with a large grin on his face. "It's MY turn!", he said and off we went. Although the distance was'nt as long, the point was proven and of a lot of good fun for all, even for the perplexed but laughing staff watching this free form humor. Dr. Branch is a well rounded individual that is very in touch with himself and the people around him. This needs no mention of his good humor and sense of play, and the heart that goes with it.

I would trust this man at the drop of my hat, and I do have a hat! While there, I purchased a fedora on the internet and had it sent to my home, to be a physical symbol of the fact that life is the greatest adventure in the universe. You need not go anywhere to find this is so, but just live it. It was an "Indiana Jones" hat. Now, Look back on what you have been told by me so far and you'll understand.

Also in this time period, Laura "Y" came to bring me to the "neuro group" and we all went through our stretching and reaching, standing and sitting, trying to enliven nerves and muscles. Laura "Y" was always surprising me by "raising the bar" beyond even where I had set it in my mind. Sometimes she would call me to task in doing antics that I thought would break me, but it was always a striving for the do-able, and testing for the areas that needed to be strengthened.

A day came, however, that I and my leg braces and sheet white "Florida Retirement shoes" were there in my wheelchair, and the neuro group was ending. Then Laura "Y" brought in a walker and had me stand. Then, with another physical therapist, and Laura's permission, I went for the "Walk Around the Block". I had finally joined.

It was like flying. After three months of being either in a bed or a wheelchair, I was on my way to a life of walking again. It was so strange to be walking a distance, even to be walking at all. And as I walked I realized the havoc of so many hours of not walking and it's effect. I paused halfway through the route to regain some strength, then continued on to the end.

In arriving back and sitting down in my wheelchair, I realized that this was my crowning moment, the delivery of my self- promise, assisted by many and helped by miracles.

I am walking. The Phoenix took flight. Nothing in my life would ever be taken for granted again.

I found all the greatest of people in life. Or, I had found out the greatness in the people in my life. Those eyes that "see" in this way was one of the gifts I had returned with from my inner journey. Many of my perceptions and wrong thinking patterns had undergone the meeting with superior realizations, new beliefs that were life changing. Many were heart based, and I now understand the statement of the Buddists that consciousness is "the clear light" that comes directly from our indwelling spirit. I had been given the opportunity to step back, and higher within myself and "see" from a lofty perch. In doing so, I became as many here in the world, but not of it, as a light bearer. On many an occasion, I have now seen the effect of standing closer inwardly to this light.

One day in the physical therapy room, I watched a woman struggle to do as I once did: To stand.

In her struggle, she did not believe that she could do such, and failed even with the help of the physical therapists. She said, "I can't do this". Sitting in my wheelchair, I suddenly piped up and said, "Sure you can! If I can do this, then you can do that!"

She then said, "All I want to do is walk with my grandchildren".

I then explained to her, "If you stand, then you are already walking in the future at some point ahead. So stand and go there!"

I came closer and watched, and she seemed to understand this explanation clearly, that she was already walking in the future if she but simply would stand. Lo and behold, she stood up. It was the love of her grandchildren, the spark and "clear light" that brought her forth. It is the spirit and unconditional love direct from God that flows through you that can surmount all obstacles.

In turning to me, the spark in her eyes showed she was feeling the exact same thing as I had felt originally. Terror with triumph, but the triumph out-glowed her fears. For someone to believe in you reminds you to believe in yourself. And "what you believe is where you are going to".

I carry not a religious viewpoint, but a spiritual one. It is clear to me that we are all the presence of God experiencing the creation and existence. But because we are all "aspects" of God and limited by our level of existence, we do not have to live up to such lofty heights such as "God". At our core He is present, and He shares the journey of life with us. We live in a time where we must re-think our beliefs and "see" with new eyes. Do not go looking for God. He is there with you.

LABORATORY 2

I stood in front of a large building set back from the road and in the country. The lawn in front was crisply cut, and there was a driveway to the left that went down behind the building. Other than a single glass door on the front, this construct was unadorned and bare. The sky was grey, as the building, and I crossed the lawn to the door and entered. I was met by a secretary in a glassed room, surrounded by extremely expensive and highly polished wooden desks and tables. All was too clean and crisp, too affluent to feel comfortable.

The secretary, a woman well dressed, led me to a door and opened it for me to enter. Walking through (and I note I was walking before I could walk) I met a man of dark and short cut hair, wearing a suit coat and tie. He would not look at me, and I could not see his face, because he constantly kept turned away from me. To my astonishment, a very large dragon made of precious metal hung in the air without any support, writhing back and forth. The room was huge, at least a hundred feet in length and fifty in width and height. Everything spoke of extreme and worldly affluence, as if that was the only value in existence. It had the feel of being void of soul and spirit. The man was not someone I actually would want to know at all. Scheming was in the "air".

It is very hard to describe the conversation that occurred, as it really was not verbal in the least bit. Not a word was spoken, but there was some form of mind–to–mind parrying. Explanation "in thought" of the huge dragon was that this man had power over it to do as he pleased, as this dragon had great power. It was not a "nice" power. I also somehow understood that I, too, had power over this dragon, even more so than the man who would not look at me. His aim was to acquire my power over the dragon to make his own power complete. This would need my total adulation and desire of the worldly riches offered. He would acquire my power and I would acquire the "things of the world" by my consent, and ONLY the things of the world. My birthright to the heavens would be void and null. It was all too clear to me that I was standing before what we call the "devil".

The insanity of this offer was compounded by the mind-to-mind nature of communication. Somehow I knew that he was unaware that I could see every thought within him. Total rejection of this offer brought a promise from him that he would make things very hard for me in this world. I doubted that, because I still had the Divine with me, and would not forsake the Heavenly treasures.

Departing, I could feel the anger and rage of this faceless man. I had retained my right and power over the dragon to resist it.

Was this a test of my loyalties and heart? I only thought of this later as I proceeded to the next "place".

I found myself wearing a long, black coat and walking through a white room of intense and brilliant light. I felt that I had been here before, but I could not remember when. In reaching the other side of the room, there was a door, of which I opened and stepped through.

I was instantly transported above the earth to a height of a thousand miles or more, to what may be called a "sky tube" that circled the Earth. It was an incredible view of the planet. It went in two directions around the Earth as two circles, crossing and joining at the top and bottom. It was made of glass or a transparent material, and the earth and space could be seen. It had a vast floor and seemed built like a mall or more refined building and went on and on in two directions, slowly curving around the planet. As I walked about, I saw people there in a very serene state, some going to and fro and others at tables or counters. Some made things and others were cooking food. Here and there were large and beautiful machines with curving lines, colored a deep, metallic blue with shining copper parts and tubes. Although I did'nt know what they did, they were gorgeous to the point of resembling jewelry.

Outside the "sky tube" on a few occasions, a thrumming noise could be heard passing, and a quick glance showed something with lights moving by. As I strolled along looking at different things, I stopped one of the people there and asked what this place was.

"From the Earth, this is the first step towards the true Heavens", this person said. It was a woman with a joyous shine to her face as she looked up and out of the "sky tube".

I walked further and came across what looked at first like an aquarium, and there were people standing about and looking at the top of it. The whole of it was the color of light and smoky jade, and on the top I could see star configurations and beautifully hand written sentences in pale white. "What are these configurations and written things that I see? What do they mean?" I asked a man standing next to me.

"These are messages sent from those who have passed higher and can see what great things are going to come to pass in existence. They send to us so that we may be informed and plan ahead accordingly", he said, adding, "They can see in time-forward, as they are slightly above time itself".

I would have stayed to read the writings, but I heard someone at distance call my name, and I turned to find out who it was. I saw a woman walking towards me. When she got closer, she looked very familiar, but I could not remember where I had seen her before.

When up close she said, "It's good to see you again! You have'nt been here in over a year!". I struggled with this, trying to remember the last time I had come, and somewhere in my memory I knew I had, but the memory escaped me. I distinctly remember knowing that I was on a level of existence above the physical and worldly of the place I had lived on Earth.

Saying hello and good bye, I walked a little further and became attracted to the thrumming from outside the "sky tube". I turned and looked up and out to see what was making this noise and saw a large object with lights, but I did'nt make out the shape. That was because as I looked, my gaze went further and beyond to the Heavens. I saw stars and nebula, galaxies and misty clouds of silver confetti reflecting the light of creation, and more than could be described. No artist or special effects could ever repeat the actual beauty of what I was seeing, and I could sense that the total of creation was filled with life out there, above and even beyond the level of existence I was visiting. I was star struck and stunned to amazement in this glorious sight. But it was time to move on.

I do not know who these people are, as a group of about four or five. The concept they had strived after has been heard of before, but they had made careful plans to keep it intact against all political and powerplay moves to abscond their creation. It was a machine of great worth and an immense step forward in the science of time and dimension. It was a machine that could fly as well as move in time or dimension. It sat vertical with a slight resemblance to a pyramid but with the sides more angled towards the vertical. It was flat on the top but for a black, squat dome and also flat on the bottom, with a horizontal and brilliant red light on each of the four sides near the bottom. It was the color of spring green. A man of about fifty with greying hair was the designer and pilot, well dressed and hugely intelligent. Several women were the "technical" crew, configuring the time and dimension plots to where they were going. With such a machine it was easy to leave and go elsewhere in time, dimension, or both, and be gone for prolonged periods of time upwards of months. Yet the machine could be configured to return and "arrive" simple seconds or only minutes after it's departure time, in spite of it being gone for lengthy voyages. They devised "body clocks" to keep tab of their true self-time and aging. Going into the future by five hundred years, they would be five hundred years old plus their age when they left several minutes ago. They would look, and be, the same age as they were five hundred years previous. In leaving for extended periods, as in several decades, they would return minutes later wearing that age that they were gone. It would seem that they aged several decades in only being gone several minutes or seconds.

It was a baffling science, and because of the aforementioned results, voyages were kept to a minimum of time gone. The true and original aim of the building of this machine was to scout out and contact civilizations on higher dimensional levels. The hope was to bring back technologies that could help planet Earth and humanity. Some problems on Earth had become so big as to threaten the very existence of the planet as well as all people.

A power grab of the machine was attempted, but the crew slipped away into dimensions. They would not have this creation of theirs "weaponized" by any party.

And as suddenly as they had vanished they returned. They had found something: A civilization of a higher scale. Peaceful and benevolent, they "gifted" the crew with some new devices that would change the planet towards the better by cleaning up the filth and chemicals and debris that was poisoning everyone. Also, a device that could eradicate many of the psychological illnesses in society.

Another voyage and the crew returned with even more startling information and knowledges. On the highest of planes they found that the Heavens were absolutely real, and they were allowed to go no further. They were sent back, being told that humanity should prepare themselves, because Heaven was coming to Earth to reclaim it, very shortly.

(8)

The Living Flame

Part of my daily routine was to gain exercise by tooling about in my wheelchair. I had not gained permission to shuffle about in a walker and with braces and the bleach white "Florida retirement shoes". It almost seemed it was a "secret" kept under wraps because it was so new and recent that I could walk, but it was understandable that I had to be careful and not fall. I could easily over-do myself and become fatigued, and to walk would mean being accompanied by someone in the medical staff. There are only so many of them to go around.

I often would come across the symbol of the Phoenix inlaid into the tiles of the floor and stop for a moment. It was artistically and aesthetically well done. Having been an artist all my life, the image found my appreciation. It was also an appropriate analogy of the process of overcoming a ruinous injury, erasing a blind and shallow view of existence and regaining one's life again. I had been through a tremendous amount, even journeyed to the doors of death, and risen from my destruction. The parallels between this "firebird" and my own life were uncanny and seemed more than mere coincidence and on many an occasion others would mention this to me. Upper worlds throw us many a hint to "look up", and the symbol of the Phoenix is timeless in it's voice to us all. Death, so-called, is followed by resurrection. I took very careful note of this so as to not slip back into a mindset of "being asleep" again in this 3D horizontal existence. A shift had happened that had set me in a very high perch. Body, mind and heart were extensions of oneself, to be looked down "through" and not to be mistaken as the root and core, which is the living flame that we truly are, within.

That "flame" that I am closer to, now, taught me of other and much higher existences. That flame is the "I", and if you look closely you will discover it as also within "you", and the cause of your conscious "being". If not distracted in mistakenly perceiving your other parts as "you", it becomes clear that you are a consciousness and personality caused by this light directly from a single source within and higher. It is the spirit and "living flame" that is unquenchable, divine and the eternal sponsor and part of us that cannot die.

That flame is what the Phoenix is and it's meaning, as a metaphor, an analogy and a fact. In short, most die and go to heaven, but some die and return with this understanding to help others and dispel the "rumor" of death. It is a passage where you "see" what I am telling you now, and the flame is clearly understood. Why do I know or believe this? Being removed from the worldly body.

It is what I retained and I learned in being whisked into a journey of such startling proportion. Being stripped of one's worldly body and then functioning on other levels was, in itself, a gift. The first hand and wholly personal knowledge that consciousness is a light from an internal source within me tore away the veil and maskings of a former, childish view. It was my time to "grow up". I "see" that it is time for the world to do the same.

You can see that this is a difficult thing to explain, and some will doubt and create an imagining in their mind and even dismiss this. But there is real distance between thinking and imagining, as opposed to having the actual experience.

Sometimes people would say, without them knowing I heard, that I had "gone through hell", and yes this is true. But in that path I also found the Heavens, both a state of being and a real and existing place. So do not fear.

The day of my departure to home was coming and felt odd to think about. After being on the rehab unit for three months total, new bonds had been formed with the staff, my "new" family that was not to be forgotten. Although a larger portion of them had not seen me walk, as tentative as it was, I saw the moment that I would revisit them and walk in, rather than be in a wheelchair.

From all medical angles, it seemed also that the "invisible tiger" had been forced back into the jungle as well and was now in remission, but certainly was to be watched carefully.

The final day arrived and Lesley came to pick me up and bring me home. It had been so long since being home that I wondered what it would be like. I truly missed the familiarity of even letting the dogs in and out and in and out, my buddy the affectionate cat that always wants to be fed, and the presence of Lesley that made home be a home. I said my good-byes to the staff and was wheeled to the main entrance, while a rush of memories of all that had been experienced flowed through my thoughts like an immense river of life. When outside, Laura "Y" locked my chair and said farewell, and I walked a few steps to the car at the curb and climbed in.

Lesley drove and I visually sucked in the world outside. It seemed so strange to be what we call "out in the public". I recognized that I was seeing with new eyes gained from the experience I had. I did not feel the same as I used to, but better.

I was learning to walk again, like a toddler, and it did'nt phase me in the least bit. ALL that had passed was worth it as a journey that taught me so much, in spite of it's cost.

Several days of settling in and a phone call from the home-visit physical therapist set the agenda to continue upward in improving my walking and strengths in that area. The PT, when she arrived, shared the knowledge that she had fifty pages of notes handed to her about me. It was obvious that a lot of people had been paying close attention to all the incredible things that had transpired.

Time progressed and so did I, as muscle and nerve responded by awakening. The progress was steep and hard, but showed continuing promise. There soon came a time for outside jaunts to a store, but Lesley knew I would not last long on my feet. There was also some apprehension in catching something "new" as in a cold or worse, and so often I was content to sit in the car like the family dog and watch the immediate world. I am never bored anymore.

Weeks before, I had abandoned the braces and the "Florida Retirement shoes", my "foot Limousines", so as to let the lower part of my legs develop more refined muscles in the calves and feet.

In my spare time, I built the cane with the brass bird's head, readying in thought and action to launch out of the walker. That time came very quickly, and again it was like being a young bird with new but delicate pinions grown and skill sets that needed sharpening. Weeks went by and very slowly the match and difference between muscle and nerves became obvious. The nerves were still seeking direction while the muscles filled in. Yet in mere months I went from learning how to stand free form to walking in public with a cane. No small feat.

The most telling of arguments towards a miracle happened when on a visit to Portland for a check-up with Dr. Aronson, one of the finest of oncologists in cancer care. In walking into the interior areas with exam rooms, he came around a corner with papers in hand and then saw me. It was the look on his face that was so precious. Astonishment and delight, surprise with some awe, he said, "My God, you're WALKING!"

Approaching me, he said, "In all my thirty five years I have not ever seen a single person overcome the type of injury you have".

He put his arm around me and said, "It's a miracle!"

I will never forget that moment, where all of us shared an astounding recognition of what had come to pass. Something uncanny had occurred and we all were part of the greatness of it.

That is why it occurred. It occurred along with other insights and grand revelations that made it into a veritable "message from the heavens" and meant for all. It brings one to believe that we live in a very special time on this planet, and on this level of existence.

Before leaving Portland, a stop at the rehab center for "show and tell" to the two "Laura's" was due. It had been about two months since I saw them. Lesley and I found them out and greeted them with the visual and physical proof that all they had done was well worth it. I stood and walked in their midst, explaining the impossibility of what had been accomplished in overcoming a permanent injury in so short a period of time. Yes, I was still lacking in some "skill sets" in walking, but that would come in time.

In this world, there are ample miracles and gifts offered to change the way things have been, and are. It is not the world that needs to change, however, but us. It will not change unless we change. To change within is a CHOICE, and when we do we automatically set in motion a change outside of us. It is so simple and pure to know this. There is really nothing to fear, as many contingencies that are invisible and of a higher nature are present to be of unbreakable help and delivery. You must have faith so that you believe so that you know. This is something that the 3D and horizontal of this level of existence shall never know, as the spiritual cannot be examined beneath a lens, condensed and put in a bottle or understood at all exept that one goes within and up. And it is something of the individual as a personal experience, becoming personally endowed. We share this through language or literature from one to another, and it never touches nor enters the 3D horizontal, but remains exclusively in the realm of being higher in nature than the scientifically provable "thing" required by scientific method. Too many times individuals have reported the same existing structure by experiencing an "inner journey" of personal nature for it to be ignored or "chortled" over, and in that is the "thing" required by scientific method. Currently, we do not remember the way of "in and up", and a near death experience, regardless of the darker tones of how or why it was compelled through an event in the physical, ends up more of a blessing than a tragedy. It becomes an insight to share, give hope, rekindle faith and belief. Remember that the greatest of insights have come from "up and within", including science itself.

The symbol, legend, mythology and concept of the firebird or Phoenix should be spoken of more. It contains clear and concise spiritual messages for those who have tasted higher realms. And in a true sense, the Phoenix still exists today. Those who have had a near death experience do go through a form of death and resurrection, but return to this level with a very important message, having been bidden to share it's content. It may be that also those who have had that experience would recognize that they have BECOME a Phoenix, proving that unquenchable living flame in us all.

LABORATORY 3

I seemed to be watching a flat screen television. The image on it was of a vast wasteland, flat and grey and stretching to immense distances and a narration spoke of it being the Gobi Desert. The narration was in two languages, one of Chinese and the other interpreting in English The view was obviously through a long distance camera lens that wobbled slightly in attempting to film this particular spot at great distance. From the left, and many miles away came an immense object that turned towards the barren waste and headed in that direction away from the viewer. It was an approximate fifteen to twenty stories in height and hinged in various places to turn, almost snakelike. It's length seemed approximately one or two miles, and it was crowned with rounded, up-side-down pie pan shaped tops with long slits in the sides. It was colored the same as the desert, the lower sides being of varying pitches with rounded corners to resemble the landscape itself. Large, military trucks drove alongside it as escorts, dwarfed by it's colossal size.

The narration explained that it was a moveable city that could roam the Gobi Desert and house an approximate one million people. It contained everything for survival and was built in case of a massive global war and invasion. Those of most importance and their accompanying staff and families would leave the cities and live, hidden, in the vast desert, within the moving city. It was built because they believed something of planet wrecking proportion was going to occur, such as a global collapse. The plan was also to set up a "kingship" and install an emperor at a later date.

I suddenly found myself far above the earth, so high as to see the entire North American continent and Central America. As I looked down, I saw that the lower half of North America was entirely covered by thick and lofty clouds from one ocean shore to the other. The cloud layer extended down and covered the land and seashores to about the middle of Central America. Many bright flashes could be seen in the clouds everywhere and at intervals.

As suddenly as I had been above the earth, I found my self down on it and in the midst of rushing winds and torrential rains that tore at green trees and bushes. Then it would subside in a lull only for another rush of wind to blast out of nowhere. It would downpour and then taper off and then another gush of rain would again fall as a torrent. Lightning flashed and thunder could be heard from everywhere. People were staying inside, but it seemed that this had started so quickly that many were caught in sudden flash floods, or had waited too long to try to make safety in their cars, and suffered dire consequences. Cars were washed away off the roads with people in them and the streets were scoured by the flooding. A small, open field had a tree in it with a road going by, and suddenly the ground burst up in a haze of red dirt as a tornado raged by from out of no where. An odd sight of a woman, dressed in an evening dress and just prior was "all dolled up" was now completely soaked, sitting on a squared stone next to a building and hanging on for dear life. She was alone with no help in sight. Small tornadoes popped up everywhere and tore at trees, while lightning bolts flashed through the sky to hit the earth with constant thunder.

On the outskirts and edge of the immense storm system, people were in cars and evacuating, attempting either to drive to a place of safety and out of the possible approach of the storms, or to get home from traveling. Hail began to fall.

A man had bought a large tract of land, south, and turned it into a resort with an Aztec theme. He had bought the land with the warm weather in mind, but recently the weather had turned atrocious, and all reports were that it might stay that way. Sunny days would suddenly turn into totally unpredictable nightmare storms of huge proportion. Nobody was going to be thinking of vacation resorts, but rather, safe areas. He was determined to sell the property, doing what the weather authorities were doing: Lie about it. However, months of candy-coating weather reports could not hide that something was amiss.

Something had shifted in the systems and gone very wrong. It was snowing hard in the Great Lakes in a large front moving towards the Northeast. It was summer. This was while the south was pounded with terrible weather. The weather stations stopped broadcasting weather reports and simply showed satellite pictures.

In Mexico and down into Central America, the same weather persisted but was made worse by the wild creatures being swept into civilized areas. Alligators, Large lizards and snakes of great proportion, along with poisonous specie, were afloat and driven by the floods into close proximity with the human population. I was shown a woman of dark hair with her child who foolishly tried to drive in her car to her home. Turning a corner, her car suddenly floated into eight foot deep waters and then was washed into the jungle undergrowth. She was accompanied by wild creatures that

Did not "think" that it was "wrong" to eat a human being. The woman's husband was elsewhere getting decidedly drunk, realized he should go and get his wife and child and began to drive to where she had been and also sank his car. He survived the ordeal, only to later find out the fate of his wife and child. The mountainous weight of his irresponsibility fell on him, but no tears or remorse would change a thing. To think right in the beginning would have stopped a lot of hell in the end. This he must live with.

I now found myself in city areas. It was dusk and very little light was shed from the city itself. No street light was working. What light was there as night came on was from the houses and building's interiors, shining out the windows. The flickering proved to be of candles and oil lanterns, showing that very little electricity was running at all or anywhere. It was also quieter than usual and lacking the traffic of the countless cars usually scurrying about. Only here and there would one be moving. It had somewhat of a calming effect at first notice, as opposed to the rushing and shouting of civilization into the darkness. It took a little more observation to realize what was truly going on with everyone.

The world had become poor, everywhere. A global economic crash had domino'ed and reached all corners of the world. Yes, some commerce was still being done in money, as in hard currency such as coins, silver and gold, but the printed money had gone the way of the dinosaur by it's worth becoming next to nothing. Hard goods transferred by barter and trade was springing up as the "new" economy, but everyone was very poor and began to realize that the "old" economy was surely to never return.

A new attitude and realization was growing amongst the people everywhere, that they truly now needed each other and each other's help. In spite of such poverty, it was welcome to embrace this recognition of each other on such a common level. Certainly there were those who would "pretend" to want to contribute while "milking" others, but they would soon be discovered out and shunned. Self-serving individuals were faced with the worst of times no matter how well they had done, because at the moment of the need of human compassion towards them they had already "burned their bridges" towards others. Reciprocation from others was to continue to be shunned by them. No one wants to be bitten twice by a snake.

It was'nt long into this world situation that news came of an odd and terrible virus that struck children only. It was spreading everywhere and wrenched the hearts of all. Their children would die, and no matter how many children they tried to have in the future, this stalking virus was now so rampant as to guarantee the death of all children. There was a cure but it was expensive, as the sellers would accept hard money only, and the cure had to be shipped a large distance. People were so poor that they had no hard currencies whatsoever, but for a few fortunate individuals who had saved such coins or had bartered early for such, or were just plain lucky.

I remember being in a cellar of a house where I supposedly lived, and I was faced with a choice. Unknown to others, I had a large pile of coinage in hard currency, a very huge bartering edge in the current times. As I looked on the pile, knowing that children were and would be dying, I weighed myself internally in the value of "what is right and wrong".

I know what it is like to love someone. I also know what it is like to lose that someone. I also know what it is like to lose someone because of death. Once a person is gone, no money can buy their return. But before that moment of "taking" happens, I clearly saw

61

that their future could be bought towards life, rather than turn a blind eye and allow their death. Not wanting to carry such a burden, I turned over what I had to the proper people who could do something and purchase the cure for many children, in the face of handing myself a risky future by doing this sacrifice, according to the times and circumstance of this dream or vision.

Only later, as I reviewed this "vision" did I again wonder if it had been a test of my heart and soul. Like the meeting with the devil. Was this a weighing of my heart and soul towards whether I would have lived or died? Or was this showing me the real value of the heart and soul in universal structure? I remembered my Guardian and the answer was clear, at least to me.

(9)

Out of Thin Air

Weeks went into months as I went from walker to bird-head cane, from the flat of inside walking to ventures out in the world. I had very quickly abandoned the walker and went exclusively with the cane. The home physical therapist in her weekly visits eventually realized a conclusion that I seemed to have all muscle groups intact and returning. We had expected that some things would not come back because of the nature of the spinal injury, but we were still getting surprises in the positive. Sometimes I would become frustrated at not feeling I was advancing quickly enough and voicing it so. Lesley would reply that I should be a bit easier on myself, because mere months before I was just learning to stand longer than a minute, and had gone through a massive experience in an ICU. That would calm me down and put "ambition versus reality" into perspective, along with my understanding of miracles.

I used to think of miracles as something that always happened instantaneously, as all I had ever heard of such seemed to be presented in this way. In the face of this was my own experience having been graciously given a series of miracles, a treasure trove of proofs of a higher and divine source that was fully aware of me, even as a small and seemingly unimportant individual in a vast universe. I had learned that if it is so with me, then it is so with all others. I had simply asked for the most basic of things, to survive, to live, to walk again, and lovingly I was given miracles. I learned to receive them, to accept them and be oh-so grateful. We all learn to give, but I have seen that we must also learn to receive with grace. Miracles are always on time, never too late nor early and do also happen over what we call time.

My first tentative walks outside the house presented the lawn with it's slopes, lumps and bumps as "rough terrain". Even with my cane I could go careening off into the pucka brush, and it was very much like walking a tight wire when it came to balance. Where once I would roam the woods, climbing over stumps and maneuver down a gulley and up the other side, there was a huge difference between what I knew how to do and what I COULD do. It was a challenge and not a nuisance, and I found some clear fascination in realizing that not long ago, I had passed through a "wormhole" and become totally new and now saw the world in a totally new way. I had also brought through that "wormhole", and near death experience, the memories of my prior life. In time, the miracle of teaching new nerves how to respond to "rough terrain" would come to pass. I saw this as living a miracle in the continuing process of unfolding.

I was new.

It was a very good thing that my sister, Cynthia, had sent me a recording device to set down the immediate memories and impressions of the inner journey. As we had talked on the phone even earlier and before the time in the ICU, she was well aware of the struggle out of some dark territories. When the major event had happened and I told her of some of the things I had witnessed, she herself had already been taking notes. She realized that those impressions would have the tendency to pop up "out of thin air" and also disappear as suddenly, and maybe permanently. Thus, the sending of the recorder. She herself recognized something of significance in the continuity of what was spoken of, something that was easily recognized as "not normal fare" when it comes to "dreams". I am almost five months removed from that period in the ICU, but some forgotten things still do come up out of nowhere and "out of thin air". When they do, I am clear of mind and under no influences of chemical restrictors and influences on what was seen. My practice of always carrying the recorder gave me instant access to noting extraneous and odd recollections as dreams, visions or stories that might not be as glamorous or long winded as some described previously. I have recognized certain dreams that were dislocations of the psyche and termed "ICU psychosis", and so have not written them, although they were very startling in themselves. But they were sure markers to become aware of the difference in texture, tone and reality between "dream" versus "vision". There is no comparison of "dream" to "vision". None.

Cynthia was a good one to bounce these "visions" off of, as she has always been a very discerning or "filtering" observer of the content of one's speech, words or story. She made no comment whatsoever questioning the bubbling well of "weirdness" coming forth from me, and that is what caught my attention. On one hand, there was the very physical brutality of a near death experience as the setting. One could automatically expect a mere and fragile human being going through a mortally threatening situation would certainly have had a "misfiring of their cylinders", so to speak.

But on the other hand, or side, there was such an uncanny line of consistency in what was seen and witnessed as stories. It was obviously beyond the scope of an invaded and dying body, mind and heart to create. Because she is family, and always was, I had to see Cynthia's reaction to this also. She would have certainly been most candid with me either way, and she was. She riveted on the nugget of truth, period.

LABORATORY 4

I found myself in a small art gallery in the city. There seemed to be no paintings. Instead, there were flat screen televisions showing unusual and highly disturbing "looped" videos, of strange creatures or men in costumes involved with dark magic, or the videos themselves were put together to induce fear in the observer by it's content. The creation of emotional reaction towards fear was considered an art form, here. But there were also hand made pieces carved of wood and assembled, either standing or hung on the white walls. I was sitting in a chair in the gallery area, and could see over into another area separated by a half wall and some vertical beams to the ceiling in darkly stained wood. There was a work table in the room beyond and younger people were gathered and discussing an upcoming event. Strangely, I did not need to hear the conversation to know what was being discussed. It was simply "in the air" and could be discerned by paying attention to it as it came out of thin air. People would talk, and their talk be heard, but their thoughts were as loud as words. I could not tell if my thoughts were like theirs, readily heard from the air.

The gallery was the site of an annual event for psychology students. Aside from psychology and being schooled in it, contributors made efforts to show or "convince" the group of other realms beyond, as in the world of spirits. They would attempt to bring forth spirits through activities to prove things beyond the physical.

But again, their leaning was of a fearful and negative nature and even towards the demonic. It might be said that it was even childish in it's attempt to impress by sensationalistic fear. Like in a twelve year old trying to scare someone with a grimace or a mask, thinking that real power was being able to cause fear.

Like the video screens, the attempt was based on fear thought of as an artform, but in this case, those contributors were actually pushing the buttons of an actual and terrifying event by playing with the demonic. Each year this was done and letters of award were given out according to their success.

In observing this, I had real aversion and discomfort of their activity. I wanted nothing to do with their antics, and the more I pulled away, the more they began to push on me to do something heinous and fearful and draw the negative. The air was thickening with a solid sense of fear as they tried to force me to do something of dark and wicked thought. It was a very uncomfortable and forced situation that was threatening to become physically violent in it's nature. I stood against the temptation to fall into fear and succumb to their wishes. And there they stood, prodding and waiting.

It was written on my face and countenance that no, I would do no such thing, and finally at a critical juncture a woman came in out of nowhere and stood by me, with raven black hair and peaceful, soft eyes and a radiance about her.

She stepped in with a complete command of everyone and scattered them away telling them to leave me be, that it was not in my ways to cause fear or imbibe the wicked or troublesome. At the same time She put off such a glow and radiance of power like a light unseen but certainly felt in presence, that all were pushed back and out of the room entirely.

On one level, the so-called physical room, all looked normal but for the raven haired woman with soft eyes. On a higher level, the woman radiated a powerful fire of divine quality.

I could see both those levels happening at once, and sometimes more, which was a strange hallmark of wherever I was in my journey. Often, several different levels could be "seen" or perceived at one time. Now, much later and only as I write this, do I suspect who the woman was: My Guardian.

That makes just too much sense.

I saw a semi-tropical setting with people that were close to the earth. They seemed to be Indonesian, Asiatic or Central American Native in their stature and build, and were having their first meetings with "modern society" and the ways of the western world. To them, the westerners were someone they could offer their presence to and be of help. Simple work brought them the exchange of money, which led to having the "things" of the western world, even sometimes allowing positions of some importance in the perceived "pecking order" of these new ways. Some of the young men took up wearing the suit and tie in their work and spent time with these new people, westerners. They began to understand the setting of price and the Parlaying for getting more goods or work for less money. But it also brought the young men into realizing the leverage they could have for getting too much for paying too little, and for often manipulating another into a corner so that they had to pay a price too steep. They learned the art of greed. These ways crept into the daily affairs of the people and began to cause bad feelings, arguments based on common needs not being able to be had for the price asked. To get as much as possible from another was the point. To help another in fairness that all may get along down the road of life was not the point. The people had been robbed of being the people to each other in the midst of this new way. Greed had brought unhappiness and poverty to the most of them, no one was poor before the new ways came, but it had now become the forced and established way. Where once they would share what they had to those of less, there was now a prohibitive price in money value to everything. Where once to have what one needed was all that was needed, now there were many "other" things considered a "need". Those who were able to dress well with clothes of the new way were considered "somebody", whereas one who dressed in the barest of need was considered "nobody", and treated that way.

In the old days and the old ways, the barest of needs were met for all, and everyone was "somebody". The people had lost their way, and even the old belief that respect, honor and dignity, consideration and care to another, simply because it was right, was pushed to the wayside. The golden rule was broken.

The men and women began to try and steal a better looking partner from another to improve their stature. This led to anger and rages by those "stolen" from and caused much violence to a severe point. The shallowness of this "how do I look" attitude towards self brought the onset of what we know as "cheating, unfaithfulness, broken relationships, mistrust, jealousy, envy".

The people were at the point of having lost themselves utterly and not being the people anymore. What you owned and what you had was what you were, rather than remembering that one was sent into life by a greater power.

Then something happened.

At first it was only a rumor, but a rumor that spread very fast amongst everyone, because they were being reminded that they were the people by a man out on the edge and periphery of the new ways. His appearance was here and there at first, rumor had it that he wore the short pants with bare chest of the old ways. Feathers in a headband and painted like a warrior with green, black and white stripes on his face and chest, sandals on his feet and blacken around his eyes. He came with a loving anger to retrieve the memory of the people and remind them back to reality. His speech was like fire in belittling those before him who thought they were "somebody" because of their fine attire. His speech was eloquent, deep and unable to be rivaled. He cajoled and ridiculed them of thinking that they were themselves the "things and acquired stuff", while strangling their real value within, that no one comes exept through the hand of a greater power that sent them. He told them that together they ARE the people and only the courageous are sent to BE the people and that no outward dressings could rival the beauty of their inner constitution and personal gifts. But they would not know their own beauty by being led into service to "things and stuff and the man-eating machine that made it". He did not need to "convince" anyone, but instead spoke the pure language of truth.

Many who had heard this and other things said were compelled to realize the truth of the matter. They began to pull away from the trappings that had caused so much havoc in their lives. Oddly, they found that by giving up a lot of the "things and stuff" of the new ways, they easily had everything that they needed, because they began to give and share as they used to. They began to call themselves "the people" again.

The new way began to suffer a domino effect. People were not buying into the "things and stuff" that were considered so important just a little while ago. All realized you could not hoe a garden with a cell phone, and spiffy sneakers did not make one a better person. With less demand for the "things and stuff", the new way began to sell those objects at a cut rate to simply keep the new way going. Soon they were sold for less cost than what it took to make them. Workers to produce the "things and stuff" had to be let go in order to "save" the new way, and became the "poor" according to that line of thinking. Many of the old ways had begun to resurface, the people remembering the ways that were closer to life and bringing them forth. In the old way, no one was poor and everyone was "somebody". No one was poor and all were cared for in that line of thinking. Of course barter and exchange occurred, but it was done with fairness in mind. And the people began to be the people again.

The painted man at some point simply disappeared, many thinking he may have been a prophet. And unknown to the people, this was a movement that was happening worldwide. They did not know that it was much harder to sustain the people where the new way had swallowed great areas into giant cities that had developed the need to ship everything in. It was a new way "need" and they had no remembrance or knowledge of the old way, but some of the old ways were beginning to seep in. The old ways were going to become the new necessity. But in the mean time the giant cities starved for the new way "things and stuff". Fighting and rioting began, rather than sharing and helping. In the face of the cities crumbling and insisting that the new way be continued, the old ways showed resilience in manipulating many of the new way "things and stuff" for the benefit of all of "the people".

I saw that something was dawning in the thoughts and awareness of "the people" over the whole world, an unusual and inner upwelling being realized in themselves individually that was actually happening to them collectively. They began to realize that some things were eternal in nature, like right and wrong that was written within us, spoken by a still, small voice.

(10)

The Fledgling

I am actually able to go for walks outside the house, with my trusted companion the "bird-head" cane. I am doing what I mentioned before, watching a miracle unfold over time. I do not take walking for granted, but see it as a blessing bestowed back upon me by a higher power. Sometimes, I am greeted by the neighbors Don and Brenda, and we say hello while they tend their yard and garden. It is beautiful. Brenda fondly calls me "gimpy" and we laugh at this, knowing without saying that it is gentle and good humored joking. We have lived enough of life to understand it. I do not know how we would have made it through the hard and harsh winter without Don and Brenda's ready help to us.

I gleefully complain at home to Lesley that my feet hurt from walking, where just a while ago I could stand on nails and not feel a thing, and before that I could not stand. Now I pretend I can walk "normal" and go through the attentive actions, and find at the end of the day there is many a muscle and joint worn and sore that I had forgotten of. I am a "toddler", a fledgling, and wear down quickly, but time will strengthen and give stamina.

Out and about in the world, at a store or in the car, or other places, I would find rushes of memory come forth of extraneous incidences. Those of most importance have been said, but some still leave me with questions. Once in a visit from Lesley and while still at the rehab center, I told her that during the night I had needed the bathroom and so got up and walked there and back, swearing on "a stack of bibles" that it was true. I was still wheelchair bound at that time. Another time while still in coma, I found myself at a house on the top floor looking out a window at the street below. It was on route one on the border of Thomaston and Rockland, with a recognized intersection. It was just before dawn, with the pale of the sky promising a clear but cold day. By the angle of the view, I knew where the house was located. After arriving home some months later and in one of our jaunts in the car, we passed through this intersection. I was stunned to find a house never noticed before that had a corner window that provided the perfect angle and view of what I had seen while in coma.

Similar scenes also came to mind in reviewing all that I could remember. Was this nonsense or had I slipped the bonds of earth for a while? Do we have another body? Psychics are supposed to be able to do these things. Is our state after "death" or transition and those accompanying "worlds" so hard to define in our worldly terms that it seems as utter fantasy?

Yes. The Universe is a very, very big place: Huge, fantastic and wonderful beyond our belief or understanding. I myself have much, much to learn, and I know now I have the time I need to learn it. Death, so-called, is no barrier.

I review being at the River Styx and the appearance of my Guardian, and in that moment everything becoming so clear, real and meaningful. ALL things made sense in that moment, and today it is the same. My Guardian appeared as the living will of God and led me back, sent me back for a reason. And I was not the same in returning. I am not ever alone and I know it. And I tell you that you are also never alone. Some must start from faith and some must start from belief but the proving of your journey will be when you KNOW.

I review the visions and see that humanity is in some dire straights with itself, and many feel on the common level no place to turn to or help to reach out for. Or do not really believe in reaching UP for. They must have faith to believe to know. Yet, that help is all around and brought forth in astounding, invisible ways. I stand and walk as proof of what I am saying, whereas I should have been paralyzed and then dead. When I came back I felt like Lazarus, so astounded. And in time I realized the meaning of the Phoenix, a symbol that showed up around me more often than a coincidence.

Often, Lesley and I discussed what would have happened if I had not become ill to the gates of death and beyond. Of course the journey would have never happened, I would possibly still be in a wheelchair, and not one message from heaven delivered for the sake of all. As I have insisted from the beginning, I "see" this as a story of not one individual, myself, but of all involved. It is everyone's story as well as mine. I also "see" that this story does not end, but will continue long after I have spoken my part.

I have a clear sense of responsibility and obligation to tell these things I have seen and witnessed. In doing so, I have often recognized the spark in the listener's eyes that says they have found verification of what they had experienced or know deep within themselves from their own lives. When they hear and then reflect on themselves, what they have experienced comes out of the realm of fantasy "shelved away" for lack of proof and becomes clearly a voice of a higher truth. Something they had seen now makes sense, and can be shared on a common but higher level of our lives. A woman took me aside once, and told me privately that she had seen an angel. Her insistence that she really and truly did was what caught my attention, as if I would not believe her. What she needed to rectify was the fact that those who "see" such things are not on a level "above" her. She was struggling with an event she felt unworthy of experiencing. I told her so, and added that it had happened to me, so why not anybody at anytime? At our very core we are a light and a spirit, none any less than another, and surely watched over in our infancy by a GUARDIAN.

I furthered this by saying that to rectify my own moment at the River Styx, I had later thought of another angle and analogy for myself. In a gigantic universe where oh so much is going on, God saw me in my death spiral and riveted His attention on me, saying, "No, that is not what I have written to be". And in telling my guardian to go and bring me out, that angel became the perfect will of God and did such that I should not perish. And in the process, I SAW it. There is nothing WRONG in seeing an angel, but everything RIGHT.

On the North American continent, there are over three million Near Death Experience people, all stories different from one another like snowflakes, yet all having the same content of certain things as a hallmark. In a sense, one is given a chance to bring "heaven down to earth", and in that journey we have all become the Phoenix. A small fraction of humanity is shown something that should be shared. Some are given the chance to realize and echo the fact of a higher guidance and existence.

I do not think that the near death experience (an NDE) stands alone. Out of Body experiences (OBE's) and the legendary "astral travel" in the other body or "Star Body" are others experiences similar that unveil upper levels of existence. All three as told to us portray the same and similar "landscape" from down here to "up there", including the lower areas of psychotic and distorted dreamings that need to be recognized and filtered out of these writings. It is like a "no man's land" or "nether world" before surfacing in a higher and organized higher reality.

Imagine being in a pond and at the bottom, seeing some light from above. In rising towards that light the bottom becomes more distant and vague, and references are lost. When we finally surface, the air we find is so much more rarified than the murky bottom, and the bottom left behind is recognized as another place entirely. There are no brilliant white clouds and the color of blue as the sky where the murky bottom exists. To us, this new and rarified place is gorgeous, and we face the problem of returning and explaining "color" to others.

I'm sure there will be NDE people that will read this material, and I felt it important to add why I chose and wrote what I did write as opposed to ALL that I had seen. Clearly seen distortions of the psyche, or rather, mind, are just THAT.

I have been graced with "accidental contact" with NDE people, and note their confusion of distorted dreaming versus "vision".

There is no comparison of dream versus "vision", and I myself found it easy to see the difference, and don't belabor myself thinking there might be some secret and hidden meaning in fractured and distorted sights.

Secondly, an NDE is not all flowers and butterflies and happy, happy. I do not blame myself for what I have seen in discarded and distorted dreamings, neither do I have the capacity to take credit for the experiences that were clearly out of my control and in the hands of something far above me. I saw the atrocious as well as the Divine, the consciousness that I was sometimes being moved in instantaneous fashion at certain points, and imbibed unusual forms of communications such as "mind to mind", and the knowing of information or knowledge out of "thin air". An NDE person will appreciate my difficulties and struggles explaining things because sometime even feelings had a "flavor", as odd as that may sound.

The most startling and surprising moment was in suddenly returning to full conscious awareness. From outside of me, I probably looked quite spacey and "not there", pitiful and sitting in a hospital bed with a food tray and oxygen tubes up my nose. From the inside of me, I "walked" in followed my blazing Guardian, and yes I say "walked", in order to follow. I saw the first rays of the sun, and in an eyeblink I was somewhere else. This time I was back.

Since then, I have still been able to find that sense, feeling and "flavor" of that lofty perch within me, above the body, above the mind and above the heart. I can fly there at will and look down upon "myself" and the world I live in.

In my returning here, I find everything far more fascinating and far more precious in it's fleeting nature of time. Those I love now, and through my life, I recognize as being part of the fleeting nature of time. All the more reason to love them now, which is the only moment we all have. The future never comes, and the past is but memory.

I returned to the world to live once more in it, because that's what human beings do, and that is what was willed for me. As to why I have returned and what I must do, I have no idea. But I see that there is a lot that can be done. Being a better person is a good start in improving the world. Being a better person makes those whose lives you are in better, and a sure influence towards the good. That will come in it's own time as part of this adventure called Life. Once I'm done here I will go elsewhere, safely, because I have seen "elsewhere" does exist: Even the Heavens.

I'm out in the "rough terrain" today, and I'm still on my feet. A couple of times I almost went careening off into the pucka brush, but my balance is much improved. I'm now leaving the bird-head cane quite often and going without it in the yard. I often "pretend" to walk normal, because if you act like it you probably will eventually be like it. Further off it's good to have a "feeler" for balance and bring the cane. I take it day by day because sometimes I'm worn and other days I'm "full of it". Yesterday I was a town away and on my own for personal business. I felt quite vulnerable as a fledgling would, even being the Phoenix.

Acknowledgments

My deepest appreciation and gratitude goes to the following people, who became very important parts of this experience and journey, on many levels. In their professional capacities they were magnificent, and in their human response even better. One of them had commented that "Everything happens for a reason".

I do agree.

Whether by self-choice or "divine script", they became woven into the very fabric of this incredible period of events.

To my darling Lesley, who stood by me and never faltered, in all that came to pass, even in the most extreme moments.

To the One God we all know, and His emissary, the Guardian.

Dr. Benjamin Branch, DO
Physical medicine and rehabilitation
MMC/Neurosurgery and Spine
New England Rehabilitation Hospital of Portland
    Laura Young, P T, MS, NCS
Physical Therapy Clinical Team Leader
New England Rehabilitation Hospital of Portland
    Laura Tardie, O TR/ L
Occupational Therapy
New England Rehabilitation Hospital of Portland
    Dr. Frederick Aronson, MD.
Oncology, Internal Medicine, Hematology
Maine Center for Cancer Medicine

Dr. Earl Ireland, Ed. D.
Psychologist
Neurobehavioral Services of New England, P C
    Donald and Brenda Pendleton
Rockport, Maine
    Cynthia Smaldone, sister
Louisville, Kentucky